Loving Your Neighbour in an
Age of Religious Conflict

of related interest

The Role of Religion in Peacebuilding
Crossing the Boundaries of Prejudice and Distrust
Edited by Pauline Kollontai, Sue Yore and Sebastian Kim
ISBN 978 1 78592 336 4
eISBN 978 1 78450 657 5

Learning to Live Well Together
Case Studies in Interfaith Diversity
Tom Wilson and Riaz Ravat
ISBN 978 1 78592 194 0
eISBN 978 1 78450 467 0

Christian Citizenship in the Middle East
Divided Allegiance or Dual Belonging?
Edited by Mohammed Girma and Cristian Romocea
Foreword by Paul S. Williams
ISBN 978 1 78592 333 3
eISBN 978 1 78450 648 3

Fortress Britain?
Ethical approaches to immigration policy
for a post-Brexit Britain
Edited by Ben Ryan
ISBN 978 1 78592 309 8
eISBN 978 1 78450 620 9

Muslim Identity in a Turbulent Age
Islamic Extremism and Western Islamophobia
Edited by Mike Hardy, Fiyaz Mughal and Sarah Markiewicz
Foreword by H.E. Mr Nassir Abdulaziz Al-Nasser
ISBN 978 1 78592 152 0
eISBN 978 1 78450 419 9

For Shoshana

With deep gratitude for our interfaith friendship

LOVING YOUR NEIGHBOUR IN AN AGE OF RELIGIOUS CONFLICT

A New Agenda for Interfaith Relations

JAMES WALTERS

Jessica Kingsley *Publishers*
London and Philadelphia

*Scripture quotations are from New Revised Standard Version Bible: Anglicized Edition, copyright © 1989, 1995 National Council of the Churches of Christ in the United States of America. Used by permission. All rights reserved.

First published in 2019
by Jessica Kingsley Publishers
73 Collier Street
London N1 9BE, UK
and
400 Market Street, Suite 400
Philadelphia, PA 19106, USA

www.jkp.com

Copyright © James Walters 2019

Front cover image source: Shutterstock®.

Library of Congress Cataloging in Publication Data
A CIP catalog record for this book is available from the Library of Congress

British Library Cataloguing in Publication Data
A CIP catalogue record for this book is available from the British Library

ISBN 978 1 78592 563 4
eISBN 978 1 78450 961 3

Printed and bound in Great Britain

Contents

Acknowledgements

This book tells the story of a new institution, so it is a story that belongs to a team of people with whom I have been privileged to work. Angharad Thain, Farhia Abukar, Daniel Coyne and Cameron Howes have all helped bring this book to fruition and continue to develop the LSE Faith Centre's work with energy and commitment. Anna Gavurin, Dr Rebecca Hardie and Dr Jacob Phillips have all made invaluable contributions to the Centre's success since 2014. Professor Craig Calhoun could not have been a greater advocate for our cause when we opened under his directorship of the LSE, and I am grateful for his mentoring in shaping the ideas in this book and its fusion of theology and the social sciences. Dame Minouche Shafik continues to champion our work and I am grateful to the numerous others in the School who have given invaluable support, including Professor Julia Black, Professor Kevin Featherstone, Dr Jan Stockdale, Susan Scholefield, Andrew Young and, perhaps most of all, Professor Janet Hartley who, as pro-director, believed that our secular university needed a centre to build relationships within and between faith communities. Bishop Richard Chartres also recognised the importance of the Centre from the beginning and continues to be unwavering in his support. Fr Earl Collins and Bishop Peter Selby have cast their critical theological eyes over drafts of this book, and HMA John Casson has helped me understand the political-religious currents of contemporary Egypt. Ophir Yarden has done much to open my eyes to the complexities of Israel and Palestine in the trips he has coordinated for our students, to which I refer at many points in the text. Professor David Ford and Professor Nicholas Adams are critical among a number of people who have inspired and nurtured our approach to interfaith relations in today's world and many of their ideas are reflected in these pages. I am indebted also to Natalie Watson who encouraged me to put all of this into words. But most of all I am grateful to the extraordinary LSE students from all around the world who have recognised the challenge of religious conflict in our age and, in spite of the multiple pressures of university life, have thrown themselves enthusiastically into programmes that have unsettled their worldviews and brought them into dialogue with difference. It is to them that this book is dedicated.

INTRODUCTION

WHO IS MY NEIGHBOUR?

2014 was a year that saw many violent conflicts around the world. There were civil wars in Syria, Afghanistan, Pakistan, South Sudan, Libya and Nigeria. But there was one conflict that drew particular international attention, and that was the Gaza War in which around 2,200 Palestinians and 66 Israelis died. It wasn't the biggest or the bloodiest or the longest conflict. But we were all aware of this violence and suffering because the Israel–Palestine conflict is a focus of interest for people in many different countries and particularly for the adherents of all three Abrahamic faiths. For Jewish people around the world, this conflict symbolises their struggle for survival in a homeland created after centuries of oppression culminating in the Holocaust. For Muslims around the world, it is the struggle for the rights of people in a land ruled by Muslims for nearly 14 centuries and which contains their third holiest site, the Al-Aqsa Mosque and the Dome of the Rock. For Christians around the world, it represents one of two things. For the ancient Christian communities, it is their fight for survival in their Holy Land as they are progressively squeezed by the Israeli state on the one hand and increasingly intolerant Islamists on the other. For millions of other Christians (primarily in the United States) who have adopted the various theologies of the 'End Times', it is a fight to secure Israel for the return of Jesus and the inauguration of a Millennial Age after the Rapture.[1] The conflict is certainly about more than just religion. But all of these religious groups have a stake in this conflict.

The world's populations of Jews, Muslims and Christians total some 4.2 billion people; that is over half of humanity. And so a conflict in this small strip of land on the Eastern coast of the Mediterranean was felt all across the globe with demonstrations from London to Jakarta, Cairo to New York. In the UK, the number of anti-Semitic attacks doubled in 2014 from the previous year. Coreligionists always feel a solidarity with their struggling brothers and sisters in different parts of the world. But that global solidarity has been reinforced by mass migration (in some cases forced as refugees), meaning that there are now significant diaspora populations from the Middle East in the West and many other parts of the world. And, of course, the dramatic change we have seen in communications technology over recent decades can bring the suffering of people in Gaza onto the Facebook and Twitter feeds of millions around the world. Social media campaigns have been accused of enflaming tensions around the world on both sides of this conflict.[2] Through both migration and technology, the global is now very local.

This local impact of the Gaza conflict in the UK prompted the Board of Deputies of British Jews and the Muslim Council of Britain to make an unprecedented joint statement in August 2014. Conscious of the passionate solidarities felt by British

---

1 These theologies are not widely understood in Europe but have wide traction in many American churches and have been popularised by the bestselling *Left Behind* series of novels by Tim LaHaye and Jerry Jenkins.

2 In October 2015 the BBC published a report on its website asking 'Is Palestinian–Israeli violence being driven by social media?' (www.bbc.co.uk/news/world-middle-east-34513693).

Jews and Muslims on each side, the statement acknowledged the deeply held opposing views about 'the origins, current reasons and solutions to end the conflict'. But it called boldly for peace between Israelis and Palestinians, and it argued that '[i]n spite of the situation in the Middle East, we must continue to work hard for good community relations in the UK'. They then used the memorable line: 'We must not import conflict. We must export peace instead.'[3]

At the London School of Economics we opened the LSE Faith Centre in the same year. The centre was originally intended to meet the practical and devotional needs of religious staff and students in the university, as well as providing new spaces for wellbeing activities like mindfulness and yoga. But from the outset we sought to adopt a constructive interfaith agenda, and that phrase of not importing conflict but exporting peace is one that has motivated me in developing our work. Religious conflicts are perhaps not something that many people thought would feature very strongly at LSE. It is a secular university founded by twentieth-century social scientists, most of whom believed that religion was being gradually eradicated by the advance of science and rational thinking. If religion would survive into the twenty-first century, they thought it would be in the form of private spirituality or as a marginal leisure pursuit. The reasons they were wrong will be explored in this book. But for better or worse (and I want to be clear I think it is both) religion has not gone away, particularly beyond Western Europe. Two thirds of LSE students come from overseas, over 150 countries in total. So many of our students have religious beliefs that they want to express faithfully on campus. Many are involved in faith-based societies and engage in all kinds of charitable

---

3   The statement was published on the websites of both the Board of Deputies of British Jews and the Muslim Council of Britain.

activities and campaigning. But many are also from countries of significant religious conflict and, just as the UK saw with the Gaza War, these conflicts inevitably get imported onto campus. Israel–Palestine is certainly a focus of much tension and activism on our campus as on many others. But we will explore later how all kinds of other grievances and conflicts from diverse corners of the world can be projected onto fellow students and lead to tensions that disrupt campus relations. As with the joint Muslim/Jewish statement, our ambitions are far greater than simply pulling up the drawbridge to keep the peace within our university community. Under the strapline of 'Interfaith Leadership for the Twenty-First Century', we run programmes that we hope will equip students to address the religious conflicts of their countries when they return home after graduation. We want to be a centre that exports peace.

The intention of this book is to share with the reader some of the lessons (both practical and intellectual) that I have learned since 2014 in setting this centre up and developing its programmes. But it isn't just a manual for university chaplains; it is intended for a much wider readership. What makes working at the LSE so interesting is that it is a microcosm of the world. We experience in our day-to-day life an intensification of the problems and relationships, ideologies and divisions that shape that world. Religion is just one aspect, but, as I shall argue, it is one of the most defining in today's world. This is the same world in which we all live, and part of the premise of this book is that our global interconnectedness – through mass migration and through communications technology – is a reality from which nobody can escape, not just those who work in international institutions like LSE. This book begins and ends with some reflections on the Parable of the Good Samaritan. That was a story told by Jesus in response to a question put to him by a lawyer: 'Who is my neighbour?' What the response to the Gaza War tells us, and what the day-to-day experience of many of us confirms, is that today our neighbour can be anyone. That may literally be the case in the sense that we cannot guarantee the person living next door to us will have been born in the same country as us, speak our language or share our faith. The mobility of the global population, both rich and poor, is reshaping communities and reconfiguring neighbourhoods everywhere. But it is more broadly the case in that the internet and communications technology are redefining global space, making our contact with people far away much more immediate. We are part of online communities as well as physical communities, and that may bring us daily into the experience of people in very different cultures thousands of miles away. Our neighbour can be anyone, our neighbour can be anywhere, and this means that our neighbour can be of any faith.

So this book is an exploration of how we might make sense of such a world and how we can be good neighbours – even loving neighbours – within the context of global religious pluralism and the conflict that sadly seems to arise from it. It is, therefore, a book about religious diversity and relations between faiths. But it is not a work of interfaith theology (as if drawing different religious traditions together into a single theological vision), nor is it a conventional theology of religions that, predominantly arising from a Christian setting, usually sought to give some positive account of how salvation might be found outside of faith in Jesus Christ. I don't dismiss this work, but, from where I stand, it does not seem to have gained much traction, and the questions it addressed seem rather secondary to the primary challenge of how we stem the tide of religion-related animosity and violence that seem to be spreading in our world. My task therefore is, in a sense, more modest. It is asking how we can think more positively of one another and how we can simply live together peacefully.

I am a Christian priest working in a social science university, and so this book is primarily the fruit of that ministry: an encounter between Christian theology and social scientific analysis. To those who think a book on interfaith relations should begin from a more religiously pluralistic starting point, I do not apologise. Part of the argument I seek to make is that two approaches to managing religious diversity are inadequate. The first is a secular oversight that gives no space to genuinely religious voices. This essentially implements an elite Western European demand that authentic religious expression be considered unacceptable in public discourse and unable to deal with diversity or disagreement. The second is a tired and equally elite Western European attempt at spiritual syncretism. It holds that religions will be united when we think of them purely as emotional/ethical responses to spiritual sentiment. As an attempt to unite the world faiths it has proved spectacularly ineffective. I argue instead for a religious pluralism in which confident religious and non-religious voices engage together in the robust but generous negotiation of healthy pluralism. So I offer this book as a Christian contribution to that endeavour and welcome responses, critiques and parallel contributions from those of other traditions.

The book has emerged out of just such expansive exchanges with LSE students and many others, for which I am immensely grateful. Some of those interfaith moments are recorded in the stories with which I open each chapter. The first does not describe events I witnessed but is the documented experience of one of the founders of Roots, an organisation in the Occupied West Bank, which I have visited with interfaith groups of students. The other stories are all encounters I have had or witnessed and learned from. I hope they give some contextual expression to the more theoretical content of the chapter.

The Parable of the Good Samaritan is one of the most familiar passages of the New Testament of which many in post-Christian societies still have some knowledge. So I hope its exploration in Chapter 1 is both familiar and also provocative in focusing on the religious otherness of the Samaritan helper as the basis for thinking about adherents of other faiths as a blessing rather than a threat. This chapter reflects on the meaning of the story within a context of a religious tribalism that is growing in our own age. It begins to raise some questions about how different faiths relate and how we can navigate both common ground and intractable difference.

Chapter 2 takes a big step back to ask the often-neglected question of why religious conflict is growing and why religious narratives are coming to the fore. It argues that the defining ideas of globalisation, which date back to the creation of the Bretton Woods institutions after the Second World War, but which were given particular impetus after the end of the Cold War, are now in crisis along with the secular assumptions that accompanied them. The politicisation of religious narratives is both a symptom and cause of these crises. That is true in the developing world to which these principles of 'liberal order' were exported but also in the West where they originated.

Chapter 3 then focuses on the experience of religious resurgence within the paradox of continuing secularisation in the Western world and an apparent desecularisation in many other regions. It then goes on to suggest that this renewed prominence of religion requires us (1) to *learn*, developing an understanding of religious literacy that explores multiple religious imaginations and (2) to *act*, both in empathetic dialogue with people of other faiths and in collective action for social transformation.

Chapter 4 returns to a more explicitly Christian perspective, seeking to give clarity to a Christian account of pluralism and offering the twin themes of *persuasion* and *curiosity* as the shaping of cultural habits and attitudes in a healthily plural society.

Finally, Chapter 5 returns to the theme of loving the neighbour and identifies some enduring obstacles in the attempt to receive the religious other as a blessing. It takes us from the recognition of the neighbour, through making space for the neighbour and receiving from the neighbour, to the point of loving the neighbour, conceiving of this love, and all attempts at building interreligious cohesion, as a theological-political act.

Religious conflict is impacting on all our lives. It is reshaping the global geopolitical order, and it is reshaping our communities. But religious conflict is not inevitable and we have many tools to resist it. What follows is a witness to some of the wisdom I have received from others and the offering of my thoughts on how the urgent task of peace between all peoples can be better understood and taken forward in our age. I hope it will be a source of encouragement and hope to those who look at the world's religious tensions with despondency, and with the fear that the neighbour who is different is more likely to be a curse than a blessing.

Chapter 1

SAVED FROM THE WAY OF BLOOD

Two thousand years after Jesus told the Parable of the Good Samaritan, another man lay wounded on a West Bank road outside Jerusalem. He was a Palestinian Muslim named Ali Abu Awwad, and he had been shot in the leg while changing a tyre on his car. It was the time of the Second Intifada, and his attacker was an Israeli Jew who lived in one of the nearby settlements, declared illegal under international law. The bone and cartilage in his knee were shattered. Both Ali and his mother had previously been imprisoned in Israeli jails, and while he recovered from the shooting in a Saudi Arabian hospital, he learned the news that his brother Youssef had been violently murdered at an Israeli checkpoint. 'How many Israelis shall I kill to heal this pain?' he asked himself. 'How many Israeli mothers have to cry to experience the salty taste of my mother's tears?' But Ali knew that revenge would not bring his brother back. It would not dry his mother's tears.

Suspicion and reluctance were Ali's understandable reaction when, some time later, an Israeli named Yitzhak Frankenthal asked to visit him and his family. Why would such a person want to visit them, a family actively engaged in pro-Palestinian struggle? Was this some kind of trap? But Frankenthal was also suffering. His son Arik had been kidnapped and killed by Hamas operatives. He was the founder of the Parents Circle Families Forum, which brings together Israelis and Palestinians who have lost family members to the conflict. To Ali this visit was a revelation. 'An Israeli mother who had lost her son held my mother's hand and both of them cried wordlessly. It was the first time in my life that I saw the other side as human beings. I saw different representatives of the Jewish people, of Judaism, and of Israelis. It had a huge impact on me.'

Ali is now an activist for non-violence and reconciliation. He is co-director of Roots, a grassroots network of Palestinians and Israelis (including settlers) who work to foster dialogue and calm tensions in the West Bank. They witness to non-violence in one of the deadliest conflict zones in the world. Students I have taken to visit their centre amidst the settlements outside East Jerusalem are profoundly affected by the experience. It is a place where, as Ali says, 'hate and suspicion are challenged and the enemy is transformed into a neighbour'.[1]

AGAINST TRIBALISM

We are all living today in a world of inescapable religious plurality. There was a time when it was possible to live in communities where virtually everybody was bound together by shared faith and religious practice. Of course, regions like the Middle East have long been characterised by religious

---

1   This story is documented in Ali Abu Awwad's April 2015 TEDxJerusalem talk *Painful hope* (www.youtube.com/watch?v=BzDEFAGv_hc) and covered by Canada's National Observer on 16 February 2016 (www. nationalobserver.com/2016/02/16/news/behind-wall-nonviolent-movement-explosive-land).

pluralism, often indeed a more healthy pluralism than we find today. But most modern societies evolved with a unifying religious identity. The historian John Bossy's depiction of Christianity in the West from 1400 to 1700 (Bossy 1985) is one of a society bound together by the rituals and narrative of shared Catholic Christian faith where non-Christian minorities are likely either to be demonised (if they live among Christians) or exoticised (if they live abroad). The loss of this religious and theological homogeneity is one of the defining features of how we live now. None of us can pretend that our own faith or belief system is the only option available. Nor can we pretend that the other options are going to go away any time soon. We no longer just learn about religious difference in school or experience it when we travel. We all live with religious difference in diverse societies. We are confronted with it daily.

To those of a cosmopolitan outlook, this religious 'melting pot' is a cause for celebration. They feel it enriches multicultural society and offers a postmodern spirituality of diverse religious fragments. We need not be constrained to one creed or confession. We can read Sufi texts, celebrate Diwali and practise Buddhist meditation. To others (perhaps the majority) religious pluralism has been a more difficult reality to embrace and may well seem threatening or unsustainable. It removes common symbols and practices that once bound our communities together. It challenges the idea of shared values or the possibility of joint civic occasions in which we can all take part. To more orthodox believers in many communities religious pluralism puts a strain on absolutist truth claims and raises legitimate questions about how we should engage with people who conceive of the world and its purpose in very divergent ways to us. Taking this premise of religious pluralism as simply a fact we must live with, we will explore in this chapter how we move beyond our fears of religious difference and become open to what God might be saying to us through it. But at the same time, we will not shy away from or gloss over the challenge of religious difference. As we think about how we can draw closer to those of different faiths, we will be reflecting all the while on what it means to hold our own faith with passion, sincerity and integrity.

One of the premises of this book is that this fact of religious pluralism has led to some quite dramatic changes in the way in which religion has been understood in public life in recent years. Later on we will explore the deep geopolitical reasons for this. But at the surface level we can say that there has been a cultural shift giving greater recognition to religion in the public sphere. The LSE Faith Centre is one example of this, where a secular university has acknowledged, for the first time, the presence of religious identities both in the world we study and in the staff and student body itself. From the believer's point of view, much of this culture change has been positive. There seems to be far greater awareness of the importance of religious faith in many people's lives. The assumption that religious people are an odd dwindling minority is far less prevalent than it was a generation ago. For me, as someone who has been working to promote engagement with and across religious traditions within a secular university, this has made for very exciting times. The young people with whom I work are interested in one another's beliefs and are rarely dismissive of them in the way that seemed to have become normal in academia at the end of the twentieth century. Much of this book is sharing these experiences in a way that I hope will be an encouragement to people who feel despondent about the future of their own religious tradition or of the constructive potential of religious faith more broadly.

But I also want to argue that the renewed presence of faith within public discourse has had some very damaging consequences for our understanding of religion. It is often remarked that our contemporary world of social media, 24-hour news channels and attention-sapping smart phones is one that is not good at dealing with subtlety, complexity and uncertainty. Our culture has a certain *reductive* effect that is impatient with complex and difficult matters. Unfortunately, religion is one feature of life that is particularly complex and difficult. Each of the world's religious traditions is a weaving together of multiple strands, and, as we shall see, those strands frequently get caught up with one another across other religions too. So religious traditions are not monolithic, and representations of religion, whether in the media or in the classroom, are frequently simplistic and generalised.

Furthermore, the complexity of religious identity is rooted in the fact that it is about more than just human cultural belongings. Most spiritual traditions have held that true faith is precisely concerned with things that are hard to pin down, even beyond human understanding. Augustine of Hippo (354–430CE) suggests that the spiritual life needs 'a pious confession of ignorance, rather than a rash profession of knowledge. To reach to God in any measure by the mind, is a great blessedness; but to comprehend Him is altogether impossible.'[2] For most of us, faith is hard to put exhaustively into words. Religious complexity is not well served by the age of the tweet and the soundbite.

To read the polemics that have been published in recent years against religion you would think that the decision to believe or not believe is essentially a straightforward, binary choice. But there is an enormous diversity of beliefs and practice across the world religions and within each tradition itself. Hinduism is a very different worldview to Islam, and the diversity within just Christianity is almost indescribably broad. Today there is

2   From Sermon CXVII (date uncertain), available at www.catholicculture. org/culture/library/fathers/view.cfm?/recnum=3330

a strong temptation to simplify all this. And many see this as the extension of a long process of the simplification of religion through the modern era as Western (mostly Christian) thinkers sought to describe and categorise religion according to common elements and shared concepts. Religions, it was decided, must have doctrines and rituals, mechanisms of redemption and priests or shamans to mediate them. Religion came to be considered as a genus of which a particular religion is a species (see Lash 1996, Chapter 1). And today, as globalisation has brought all these traditions into a more intense interaction than ever before, the temptation to reduce the complexities of religious difference in the public mind is overwhelming.

So one of the troubling effects of this increased discussion of and provision for religion has been a taking for granted that, when we talk about religion in public life, we all know what we're talking about! When governments seek to 'engage with faith communities', when universities seek to 'make provision for religious observance', when religion and belief becomes a 'protected characteristic' within equality legislation, there is an inevitable process of homogenisation. Governments need a clear set of representative leaders to engage with. Universities need a clear understanding of what the religious requirements may be of each faith group. Lawyers need clear definitions of what beliefs are and what status they have in law. Consequently, we have lost sight of the complex, multifaceted stories that each faith tradition tells and have come to think of religions as rather more like tribes.

Tribes are easier to understand. Each tribe has its tribal chiefs. Each tribe has its beliefs and rituals that bind it together. And tribes, of course, make clear distinctions between 'us' and 'them' that cause us to view members of other tribes with suspicion and fear. The perception that religions are tribal groupings, prone to violent confrontations with one another, is deeply embedded in Western European history. Responses to the Early Modern Wars of Religion instilled the belief that innate religious violence must be suppressed by secular authorities. Religion came to be viewed as a dangerous force that must be contained by institutions that consider themselves to be religiously neutral (Cavanaugh 2009). That thesis will be challenged in various ways through this book. Yet those of us who do hold religious faith need to acknowledge with some humility how much tribalism appears to be capturing the religious imagination of so many around the world today. In many regions that have lived with religious plurality for centuries, minorities are now being viewed as a threat. That is true in much of the Middle East where Christian communities that have existed since the earliest times are being pushed out by a violent form of Islam. As the so-called Islamic State spread through Syria and Iraq, Christians were told to convert to Islam, flee or be killed. Of those who have left most are unlikely ever to return. But the problem of religious tribalism isn't just owned by one religion or one region of the world. Hindu nationalists in India and the Buddhist majority in Myanmar are all turning against the minority faiths within their societies. Even in our predominantly Christian culture we see a rise in tribal attitudes towards non-Christian minorities. Terrorist attacks have created a surge in hate crime directed towards Muslims and a former openness towards other faiths appears to be superseded by the sense that Christian identity is now under threat in a multifaith society.

One danger of talking about religious 'tribalism' in this way is that this word is often associated with a non-Western primitivism, and that might tempt us to see this problem as essentially an external one. As Canadian philosopher Will Kymlicka explains:

> Resistance to multiculturalism is attributed to pre-modern identities and attitudes of 'tribalism' [within societies which]

lack the political sophistication to deal constructively with issues of diversity, and so cannot appreciate the merits of the models of multiculturalism that have emerged within 'mature' Western democracies. (Kymlicka 2007, p.20)

This enables people (particularly those who had assumed the inevitable eradication of religion by the spread of post-Enlightenment reason) to interpret the 'importing of conflict' that I described in the introduction as the intrusion of a foreign and primitive mentality for which we enlightened Westerners are not responsible. This thinking is wrong for two reasons.

First, we are seeing more and more public recognition of how the religious (and other) conflicts of the wider world are not something from which the stable Western world has sought to insulate itself, but frequently something that we have stoked, provoked and often caused. As we pass the one hundredth anniversary of the Balfour Declaration, the example of the Israel–Palestine conflict is a striking example. This is a story of European and American interaction. Western intervention in the Middle East up to the Iraq War and beyond has contributed in various ways to the resurgence of religious violence. So as we come on to discuss the Samaritan who helps the victim of a robbery and ask whether we can overcome tribalism with acts of charity, we might also ask whether we share some complicity in the initial injustice.

Second, we should not underestimate the 'tribal mentalities' of our own Western culture and way of life. A theme revisited several times in this book is how Christianity (or at the very least post-Christian culture) is implicated in a Western mindset that is not as outward-looking or conducive to pluralism as it might be. We are all complicit in today's religious tribalism: Western and non-Western, Christian and non-Christian.

Part of my motivation in writing this book is my conviction that tribalism is antithetical to the Christian worldview. Bishop Peter Selby writes:

> The Church is not a tribe, but a new kind of people. It offers to humanity the possibility of membership in a new kind of community, open to new possibilities, relying for its existence on God's free and gracious act. Yet it often does not seem that way. (Selby 1991, p.56)

Christians lapse into tribalism too. But, in its essence, Christianity is a force that should work against all forms of human tribalism. We will explore how this is so and how authentic Christian living should be expressed through love of neighbour in our very troubled and chaotic times. Others can speak for their own faiths, but my experience of working in interfaith relations over many years, including with inspiring people like Ali Abu Awwad, has suggested to me that other religious traditions also have resources that work against the sectarian mentalities that appear to be gaining ground across the board. The Qur'an addresses the theme of tribalism again and again, reflecting the role that early Islam played in uniting the diverse factions on the Arab Peninsula. The Sura of the Family of Imran exhorts believers to 'Hold fast to God's rope all together; do not split into factions. Remember God's favour to you: you were enemies and then He brought your hearts together and you became brothers by His grace' (3.103). Muhammad's continuing desire to maintain good relations with those who did not convert from Judaism and Christianity but remained 'People of the Book' reflects how this anti-tribal instinct extends beyond religious boundaries too.

There are many biblical texts we could draw on to explore this theme. But Ali's story resonates with one of the most famous stories Jesus ever told. The Parable of the Good Samaritan is very familiar to both churchgoers and non-churchgoers, and yet it is most commonly interpreted superficially as a remarkable illustration of selfless generosity. It is certainly that. But it has much more to tell us about the dangers of religious tribalism and how Jesus scandalously undermines it.

GOOD SAMARITAN

Just then a lawyer stood up to test Jesus. 'Teacher,' he said, 'what must I do to inherit eternal life?' He said to him, 'What is written in the law? What do you read there?' He answered, 'You shall love the Lord your God with all your heart, and with all your soul, and with all your strength, and with all your mind; and your neighbour as yourself.' And he said to him, 'You have given the right answer; do this, and you will live.'

But wanting to justify himself, he asked Jesus, 'And who is my neighbour?' Jesus replied, 'A man was going down from Jerusalem to Jericho, and fell into the hands of robbers, who stripped him, beat him, and went away, leaving him half dead. Now by chance a priest was going down that road; and when he saw him, he passed by on the other side. So likewise a Levite, when he came to the place and saw him, passed by on the other side. But a Samaritan while travelling came near him; and when he saw him, he was moved with pity. He went to him and bandaged his wounds, having poured oil and wine on them. Then he put him on his own animal, brought him to an inn, and took care of him. The next day he took out two denarii, gave them to the innkeeper, and said, "Take care of him; and when I come back, I will repay you whatever more you spend." Which of these three, do you think, was a neighbour to the man who fell into the hands of the robbers?' He said, 'The one who showed him mercy.' Jesus said to him, 'Go and do likewise.' (Luke 10.25–37)

Tribes hold together through conformity to shared codes and a clear identification of who is inside and who is outside. Human beings are social animals, but the societies within which we seem to feel comfortable are not limitless. They need laws, customs and shared identity that require policing. The lawyer in this story is powerful within the hierarchy of his religious tribe because he is knowledgeable about the shared code, a scholar of the law, and he seems suspicious about Jesus' commitment to the tribe. We are told that his question was not an innocent one but intended to put Jesus to the test. Jesus deflects the interrogation with a question, and the lawyer is able to demonstrate his knowledge of the Jewish law. So Jesus praises him, but the lawyer is still not satisfied that Jesus is to be trusted and he continues his interrogation.

The question he asks is revealing. He does not ask about the first commandment, 'You shall love the Lord your God.' He does not wish to consider such questions as 'But who is God?' or 'But what does it mean to love?' These are the theological questions that take us deeper into the nature of faith. But as religion becomes more tribal, they are asked less and less often. I once had a conversation with a priest who had become involved at a senior level in efforts to initiate peace talks in the Middle East. As we discussed complex ways in which religion has become caught up in so many of the world's violent conflicts, he remarked, 'The paradox is that everyone is talking about religion, but no one is talking about God.' So the lawyer avoids these challenging topics and asks, 'Who is my neighbour?' It is a profoundly tribal question. Who is to be trusted? Who can be befriended? Who is in? Who is out? Who do I not need to love? And if the lawyer asks, what is for him, the easy question, then it seems initially that, as Jesus begins telling his story, he will give an easy answer. He tells the story of a man who has been assaulted and is in clear need of life-saving help. We can all see that the neighbour will be the one who comes to the rescue. And this is true. But as the story unfolds, it becomes not just about the *action* of the neighbour, but also the *identity* of the neighbour.

The first two people on the scene are custodians of the religious code that define the tribe and they are shamed by their failure to help the man. The sacrificial rituals of the Temple in Jerusalem are at the heart of the life of the Jewish people and the means of their reconciliation with God. The priests of the ancient Cohen tribe were those who administered the sacrifices in the Temple, and the Levites were those who assisted in this worship. Jesus' casting of them in this story is typical, therefore, of his criticisms of the religious hierarchy throughout the gospels. We are told that the chief priests and the Pharisees themselves understood that his parables were frequently directed against them (Matthew 21.45). But this naming of the sacred castes of Jews – priests and Levites – is particularly provocative because it raises the question with regard to Temple worship: what is all this religion for? The story is being told to illustrate the meaning of the central commandments of the Torah: love God, and love your neighbour as yourself. But Jesus accuses those who are supposed to be most committed to the divine law of failing to fulfil it. Some interpret the story as an explicit illustration of the kind of religious hypocrisy he saw in the overzealousness of the Pharisees. Priests and Levites were restricted from having any contact with the dead, which would compromise their ritual purity. So these two passers-by may have decided not to get too close in case the injured man was already a corpse. Or they may have just been afraid. The road from Jerusalem to Jericho was known as 'The Way of Blood' because of the notorious dangers posed by bandits and robbers. So they may have feared that this brutal assailant was still around or that the victim himself was an assailant in disguise, waiting to trick them.

But if this was an excoriating attack on the religious elites of the tribe, the story was also unfolding in a formula that Jesus' hearers would recognise. Most cultures like to make jokes at the expense of the people in charge, and it seems likely that this threefold pattern of storytelling was well established. First came the priest. Then came the Levite. But what Jesus' audience would have been expecting next would have been themselves, the ordinary Jew. They are anticipating the message that the leaders of their tribe do not behave as the neighbour, but *they* would. It is as if Jesus is building them up to have their tummies tickled, only to slap them in the face.

The Samaritans were despised. It is hard for us fully to understand the connotations these days given how 'Samaritan' has entered our lexicon as simply meaning 'a person who does good'. In the UK, the Samaritans is a wonderful and well-known charity that provides a supportive ear to people in the depths of despair. Countless sermons and school assemblies have extolled us to be a 'good Samaritan' in a way that has made this phrase sympathetic and cosy. So it is almost impossible for us to conceive of the disdain, loathing and fear that Jesus' hearers would have felt at the unexpected casting of a Samaritan as the hero of this story. We perhaps have some clue at the end of the encounter when Jesus forces the issue by asking who the neighbour is in the story and the lawyer seems unable even to utter the word 'Samaritan', saying only 'the one who showed him mercy'.

Samaritans were despised for reasons of religious difference. Samaritanism still exists today and is a religious tradition closely related to Judaism, but has had variable, sometimes violent, relations with it. Tradition holds that the split occurred at the time of the priest Eli who mentors the young prophet Samuel in the third chapter of 1 Samuel. Relations between Judeans and Samaritans were not always bad. The fact that they shared the Pentateuch (the first five books of the Bible) illustrates some ongoing dialogue and common spiritual life as these texts became fixed. But the immediate centuries preceding Christ seem to have witnessed deteriorating relations. Small changes were made to the Samaritan Pentateuch that reflect sectarian divisions. These are reflected in Judean texts of the period too, such as a reference in the Book of Sirach (second century BCE) to 'the foolish nation that lives in Shechem', commonly held to refer to the Samaritans.[3]

But their main point of divergence, which came to the fore over this period, was the location of the site of sacred worship that is referred to in the Book of Deuteronomy as the place where sacrifices must be offered to God. We read in John's Gospel of Jesus' conversation with a Samaritan woman who says, 'Our ancestors worshipped on this mountain, but you say that the place where people must worship is in Jerusalem' (John 4.20). The mountain she is referring to is Gerizim near Nablus. Samaritans believe this to be the sacred centre of Israel since the time of Joshua whereas the Judeans (of whom Jesus was one) believed Mount Zion in Jerusalem to be the resting place of the Ark of the Covenant and built their great Temple on this site.

So we can see again how the juxtaposing of the Samaritan with the priest and the Levite (who worked in the Temple in Jerusalem) is rubbing salt in some very specific and open wounds. Jesus' response to the Samaritan woman makes clear that the location of the Temple is ultimately of no consequence, but to Jesus' hearers it was a major point of contention between the two religious tribes. Their temple, serviced by the priests and Levites, was the bedrock of the Judeans' relationship with God. The Samaritans opposed this

---

3   The origins of this split are comprehensively set out in Knoppers (2013).

and were despised for it. So hostility between Samaritans and Jews was not just the result of ethnic division; it was one of religious disagreement. As Nick Spencer observes in his enlightening survey of political readings of the parable, 'it was precisely in *religious* difference – practices of worship, interpretation of texts, attitudes to ritual commands, to assimilation, to syncretism – that the core bitterness of the Israelite–Samaritan dispute lay' (Spencer 2017, p.122).

So, yes, Jesus is telling the lawyer and the crowd that loving your neighbour means helping someone in need. But he is using this fairly obvious moral lesson to say something far more challenging about where that neighbourliness might come from and where we might be challenged to overcome our perennial instincts to religious tribalism. Twentieth-century interpretation of Jesus' parables has tended to insist on a single meaning to each parable and a single moral injunction (see Dodd 1955). But we can already see that in this case the simple moral injunction – don't ignore those in need – is accompanied by other moral challenges about religious hierarchy and interreligious prejudice. That modern, primarily Protestant, approach to interpretation was kicking against the pre-modern tradition of interpreting parables as very elaborate allegories in which the simple, most important, meaning might easily be lost.

The Parable of the Good Samaritan is the most often cited example of this approach. Early Christian thinkers such as Origen, Ambrose and Augustine did not just regard the parable as a lesson in moral teaching but saw each element of the story as a symbolic illustration of the entire narrative of redemption. This, for example, is Origen's reading:

> The man who was going down is Adam. Jerusalem is paradise, and Jericho is the world. The robbers are hostile powers. The priest is the law, the Levite is the prophets, and the Samaritan

is Christ. The wounds are disobedience, the beast is the Lord's body, the *pandochium* (that is, the stable), which accepts all who wish to enter, is the Church. And further, the two *denarii* mean the Father and the Son. The manager of the stable is the head of the Church, to whom its care has been entrusted. The fact that the Samaritan promises he will return represents the Saviour's second coming. (Origen 1996, p.138)

So the most confusing thing about the allegorical interpretation, and what sits uneasily with the modern approach to parables, is that the person who does what Jesus tells us to do (the Samaritan) is, in fact, interpreted as Jesus himself. Augustine believed that the parable is not simply telling us how to behave; it is telling us something about God:

> God Himself, our Lord, desired to be called our neighbour. For our Lord Jesus Christ points to Himself under the figure of the man who brought aid to him that was lying half dead on the road, wounded and abandoned by the robbers. And the Psalmist says in his prayer, 'I behaved myself as though he had been my friend or brother.' (Augustine 2004, p.531)

So the lawyer may have asked the easy tribal question 'Who is my neighbour?' But, according to these earlier interpretations, the more complicated theological questions 'Who is God?' and 'What does it mean to love?' are in fact being answered. To love God is not to love a remote cosmic figure; it is to love the one who comes to assist us. And to love our neighbour is not just to assist others in the pattern of Jesus Christ but to be open to receiving the loving assistance of those we do not like. If this is a part of Jesus' intended meaning, it is not the only occasion that he uses parables to identify himself with the outsider and play with our sense of who exactly is *giving* and who is *receiving* in acts of charity. In the Parable of the Judgement of the Nations, Jesus identifies himself with a range of outsiders who many would have viewed as being judged by God for their misfortune or, in the case of the stranger, outside of the sphere of tribal responsibility. 'Truly I tell you, just as you did it to one of the least of these who are members of my family, you did it to me' (Matthew 25.40).

The great Protestant theologian of the twentieth century Karl Barth therefore comes to the perhaps unexpected conclusion that 'the primitive exegesis of the text was fundamentally right. [The neighbour] stands before him [the victim of the robbery] incarnate, although hidden under the form of one whom the lawyer believes he should hate, as the Jews hated the Samaritans' (Barth 2010, p.122). The story is full of inverted expectations. The religious leaders are those failing to fulfil the Law. The despised outsider is the neighbour. And the person who is believed to be ungodly is, in fact, a manifestation of God. In order to understand all this, Barth sees the lawyer as having to undergo an inversion of his own power and authority. He has to see himself, not as the one who proves himself to be the good neighbour, but as the one in need of a neighbour:

> All very unexpected: for the lawyer had first to see that he himself is the man fallen among thieves and lying helpless by the wayside; then he has to note that the others who pass by, the priest and the Levite, the familiar representatives of the dealings of Israel with God, all one after the other do according to the saying of the text: 'He saw him and passed by on the other side;' and third, and above all, he has to see that he must be found and be treated with compassion by the Samaritan, the foreigner, whom he believes he should hate, as one who hates and is hated by God. He will then know who is his neighbour, and will not ask concerning him as though it were only the matter of a casual clarification of a concept. He will then know the second commandment, and consequently the first as well. He will then not wish to justify

> himself, but will simply love the neighbour, who shows him
> mercy. (Barth 2010, p.221)

So we see that what has often become a sentimental story of compassion for an injured man is in fact a story that wants to take us on a transforming journey. We ourselves are on the Way of Blood, caught up in the patterns of religious tribalism and abuses of power that so easily lead to hatred and violence. We may console ourselves with the potshots Jesus takes at religious leaders who turn out to be less virtuous than they think. But we are not the third person to come along the road and claim the heroic role of saviour figure for this poor misfortunate. We are the one lying half dead in the road, and neighbourliness comes to us from the most unexpected quarters. It comes from the religious other. It comes from a member of another tribe.

ENCOUNTERING GOD IN THE RELIGIOUS OTHER

The theme of encountering the love of God in the outsider – the other – has not, of course, been entirely neglected in the exegesis of the Parable of the Good Samaritan. Many Christian advocates for different forms of equality have sought to recover our awareness of the otherness of the one whom Jesus identifies as the neighbour in this parable. Martin Luther King Jr., in his famous 'I've been to the Mountaintop' speech, describes the Samaritan as 'a man of another race', who is able to see beyond racial divisions. 'He had the capacity to project the "I" into the "thou," and to be concerned about his brother.' Jesuit priest and queer theologian John McNeill retells the story with the Samaritan as a gay drag queen who comes to the aid of a man on 42nd Street in New York City who is ignored by a Catholic priest and a social worker (McNeill 1988, p.96). And before the 2015 UK General Election, the bishops of the Church of England read the parable in the context of increasingly hostile attitudes towards migrants to emphasise the Samaritan as 'the foreigner' and 'member of despised social group' (House of Bishops 2015, p.43).

But the idea of the *religious* otherness of the Samaritan is perhaps more challenging. It is as if we find it easy to say that the black person or the gay person or the unwelcome foreigner can be a good Christian too. But can it be possible for Christians to affirm somebody who is not a Christian in their religious otherness? Even more than that, can we go as far as this parable implies to say that a person of another faith is witnessing to God more effectively than if they held our own faith? That would seem to be compromising or heretical. It would seem to imply that religious beliefs do not matter, that you can believe what you like as long as you are a good person. I do not believe that, and I don't think it is what Jesus is saying in the parable.

This book is about how people of different religious commitments can love and live alongside one another while not compromising their beliefs. And my experience of working in interfaith relations has been that many people have become allergic to the word 'interfaith' because of this imposed idea that, at the end of the day, doctrine and religious practice do not matter as much as some common spiritual and moral essence. According to this perspective, what Jesus is teaching in the parable of the Good Samaritan is that the theological disputes between Jews and Samaritans are of no consequence. The practical expression of love is all that God is concerned about. In his book *The Limits of Religious Tolerance*, Alan Jay Levinovitz argues that this idea has ultimately been a way of creating a shortcut in the tricky business of forging religious tolerance in multifaith societies. It is rooted in the rise of modern secular states that relegated religion to private life and, in so doing, gave all religious positions a kind of equivalence. 'To make tolerance easier,' Levinovitz writes, 'some popular authors and academics preach a comforting vision of religion that renders argument unnecessary, viz., all religions are essentially the same, and therefore fundamentally compatible' (Levinovitz 2016, p.11).

We will return to the problems raised by this kind of syncretistic approach in Chapter 3. But to conclude our exegesis of the Parable of the Good Samaritan we need to consider two aspects of the religious difference presented to us in the story. The first concerns the nature of the religious difference at stake and the potential dangers of extrapolating too much from it. It could be argued that the Samaritans were not a 'proper' religious other but rather the result of a schism within the Israelite tradition. We might say that their theological disagreements were more those between denominations of one faith rather than across different religions. This parable therefore addresses *intrafaith* difference rather than *interfaith* difference.

It is certainly the case that the disagreements within a religious tribe can be far more vociferous than those with whom we have never considered a mutual belonging. Subtle differences in theological understanding can often pose a far greater challenge, because they seem to undermine our own spiritual understanding and sense of what we hold in common. Notions of loyalty and fidelity are integral to the survival of the tribe, so the accusation of treachery can be ferocious against religious dissenters. In his comprehensive survey of religious tolerance in the West, Perez Zagorin describes the evolution of the concept of heresy within the Christian tradition and the sophisticated (often gruesome) infrastructure that was created by the medieval church to police it. Frequently Christian heretics were viewed as far more dangerous than adherents of other faiths. 'Jews and Muslims were…regarded as alien Others and enemies of Christ, but the heretic differed from them in being a Christian who had betrayed his baptism and separated himself from the church' (Zagorin 2003, p.43).

But the distinctions between intrafaith and interfaith are not as clearly defined as might first appear and have, again, been reinforced by the modern reduction of religions to discrete monolithic tribes. Christianity itself is, after all, the result of a schism within the Jewish tradition. Early Christians may have identified with this parable because they had become the new Samaritans in the sense of a minority group who were, as we learn from John's Gospel, 'thrown out of the synagogues' (John 16.2) and persecuted. They were the despised religious other, and the association of Jesus with the Samaritan in all early interpretations would be seen as one expression of his words, 'If the world hates you, be aware that it hated me before it hated you' (John 15.18). Scholars differ about the extent to which Islam too should be seen as a derivative strand of the Abrahamic tradition, but it is certainly the case that we share many Bible stories and prophets, including devotion to Jesus. In the Eastern faiths, the notion of different religions as discrete tribes breaks down even more quickly with Hinduism, Sikhism, Jainism and Buddhism sharing much common heritage, philosophy, practices and beliefs. It might be better to think of the different religions we speak of today as being cousins within the same families, rather than unrelated tribes.

In any case, Zagorin's thesis is that the toleration of dissenters within one tradition is inextricably linked to the provision of a wider religious freedom. 'Wherever tolerance has been recognised as more than a temporary expedient, wherever it has been advocated for religious, moral and humanitarian reasons, it has also had a relation to and tended to develop in the direction of religious freedom' (Zagorin 2003, p.311). Essentially, the advocates of religious toleration were arguing that adherence to spiritual truth must be entirely free of coercion. In the West that evolved from a rejection of violently enforced uniformity in Christian life to a rejection of coercive participation in the Church altogether (something previously experienced by many non-Christian minorities, particularly the Jewish people). So the Samaritan may be closer in doctrine, practice and scripture to the Jew than the Zoroastrian or the Hindu; but the Samaritan's representation of broad religious otherness in this parable holds, and its use in exploring God's presence to us in those of other faiths is a natural extension.

The second issue to address is perhaps more challenging and gets to the heart of the tension that this book is seeking to explore. I am asking whether this parable can help us think about how people of one faith can relate to those of another. As a Christian commenting on a Gospel story, I am, in the first instance, asking whether it helps us think about how Christians relate to non-Christians. But this whole story takes place, by definition, in the pre-Christian era. Does the lesson about the religious other that Jesus appears to address to his initial hearers necessarily, therefore, apply to his later followers? As we saw, in her conversation with Jesus by the well, the Samaritan woman gets to the heart of the issue at stake in the religious difference between Samaritans and Israelites: the correct location of sacrificial worship (John 4.20). Jesus' response appears to include an affirmation of his Judean perspective: 'You worship what you do not know; we worship what we know, for salvation is from the Jews' (John 4.22). But he then suggests that soon this historic disagreement will be irrelevant. 'The hour is coming when you will worship the Father neither on this mountain nor in Jerusalem' (John 4.21). This is one of a number of allusions in the gospels to the idea that Jesus himself will replace the Temple and that his risen and ascended body will make it possible for all people, in all places, to worship God in a new way: 'The hour is coming, and is now here, when the true worshippers will worship the Father in spirit and truth' (John 4.23). In other words, Jesus does not resolve the religious disagreement about the location of worship. Rather, in himself, he supersedes the religious difference.

Does this mean, therefore, that Jesus' apparent championing of the Samaritan in the parable is only possible because he is about to nullify the religious difference that the Samaritan represents? Is it really a case of 'a plague on both your houses', because the new Gospel of Jesus will leave both these religious positions outdated and futile? And here's the rub in interfaith relations. Because, to a large extent, the Christian answer to these questions is 'yes'. This *is* the claim of the Gospel: that temple worship as both Jews and Samaritans conceived it is now unnecessary; that all people can be made acceptable to God by Jesus' death and resurrection through the power of the Holy Spirit poured out at Pentecost on people of all nations, tribes and languages. This has prompted many Christians to say that our faith has little to say about religious difference because it is not really a religion at all. Some of my favourite twentieth-century theologians – Karl Barth, Dietrich Bonhoeffer, William Stringfellow – have developed the theme that the Gospel of Jesus Christ is the overturning of religion *per se* with precisely such divisive practices as cultic worship and dietary laws that cause 'religious' people to lapse into tribalism and degenerate into adversarial tribal behaviour.

And yet some humility is required here. Christians have to ask what this powerful, religious-difference-overturning Gospel has caused us to believe and caused us to do. Because the flipside of a universal Gospel beyond religion for all people can be a worldview that itself permits for no outsiders. A totalising inclusion can easily become a totalitarian rejection. If we think we can stand above such petty interreligious squabbles as preoccupied the Jews and Samaritans, we delude ourselves. Our Gospel may be one of universal embrace, but its practitioners have, history suggests, been most inclined toward exclusion. The eighteenth-century French philosopher Voltaire recognised this paradox that 'of all religions, the Christian is without doubt the one which should inspire tolerance most, although up to now the Christians have been the most intolerant of all men' (Voltaire 1764/1924).

The problem outlined here is sometimes referred to as 'supersessionism', and it has long been the major stumbling block in Jewish–Christian relations. European Christians have an appalling history of persecution of the Jewish people. Numerous Councils of the Church restricted the rights of Jews, from the banning of intermarriage (Council of Chalcedon in 451) to the enforced wearing of a Jewish badge that pre-empted that imposed by the Nazis (Fourth Lateran Council in 1215). Beyond the fatuous accusation that the Jews were the murderers of Jesus, Christians have found the enduring presence of Jews difficult to live with precisely because of our claim to supersede them. We argue that their covenants with God through Abraham and Moses have been replaced by our 'New Covenant' that has extended God's promises to all people. Only after the Holocaust at the Second Vatican Council did the Roman Catholic Church qualify its position on this issue, stating that 'Although the Church is the new people of God, the Jews should not be presented as rejected or accursed by God, as if this followed from the Holy Scriptures.'[4]

But supersessionist moves are an obstacle to interfaith relations from a number of different quarters. They are problematic precisely because they tend to form a double move of *appropriation and supersession*: I adopt and give meaning to your tradition (which may diverge greatly from your own meaning) but add an important new dimension,

---

4   Declaration on the Relation of the Church to Non-Christian Religions, *Nostra Aetate*, proclaimed by His Holiness Pope Paul VI on 28 October 1965.

which I claim that you fail to understand. So we say to the Jews, 'We share your scriptures and your understanding of God in the Old Testament [so we think], but you have failed to grasp this important new development, the coming of the Messiah in Jesus.' I only really understood how frustrating this line of reasoning can be when I realised this is effectively what Muslims can end up saying to Christians: 'We share your prophets and we even believe in Jesus too [though quite differently to Christians], but you have failed to grasp this important new development, the revelation of the Qur'an to Muhammad who is the final prophet.' Eastern religions too can make appropriating and supersessionist moves. I once attended a frustrating Hindu–Christian dialogue where our Hindu friends kept repeating that they were more than willing to embrace Jesus as an emanation of Brahman (alongside their 330 million other deities!), so why were we being so unwelcoming of their pluralist approach?

So we have a tension here. Holding on to our own tradition with integrity is likely to involve some form of supersessionist claim. Yet while such claims are nearly always intended to be an expression of universal embrace, it is precisely these claims that are most dismissive of other traditions and make us deaf to what people of other faiths are really trying to say to us. So there will inevitably be an element of supersessionism in the Christian's interpretation of the Parable of the Good Samaritan. In the end, Jesus wants us to be neither Jews nor Samaritans but people who live by his Word in spirit and truth. But he still presents us with this challenging lesson of God's loving presence manifest in a neighbour who is a despised religious other. We are complacent and sanctimonious if we think that lesson was intended only for the lawyer in the story. As Karl Barth suggests, the parable is a call to all of us to be on a journey of humility, relinquishing our moral superiority and recognising that God may be speaking to us – even seeking to heal us – through those whom we hold in contempt for their religious difference.

Ali's story at the beginning of this chapter reminds us of an excellent case in point. Like the dispute between the Jews and the Samaritans, the conflict between the Israelis and the Palestinians often focuses on the Temple. Particularly since the Second Intifada, tensions have focused around ownership and access to the area that Jews call the Temple Mount and that Muslims have, since the seventh century, called the Haram al-Sharif or 'Noble Sanctuary'. Some Jewish extremists want to rebuild the Temple that the Romans destroyed in 70CE, restoring the religious centre of the state of Israel as it was in ancient times. Jewish texts have always called for the rebuilding of this temple on this site, and it is that theology that is driving much Zionism (of both Jewish and Christian forms) today. But the same site holds deep significance for Muslims too. It is the third holiest site in Islam, the original *qibla*, the direction towards which Muslim prayed before they switched that to Mecca and the site from which Muhammad is believed to have ascended into heaven. We will look again at the significance of this site in Chapter 3.

The Christian temptations towards smug supersessionism are great here. We may hear Jesus' words to the woman at the well that we will no longer worship on this mountain but in spirit and in truth and see ourselves as above these outdated religious squabbles. But the ugly truth is that Christian involvement in this part of the world has been among the most violent and divisive. The multiple Crusades that butchered Jews, Muslims and even other Christians in this region lend little credence to the view that Christians have all the answers to the problems of religious difference. The powerful force of Christian Zionism today serves only to inflame further the tensions on precisely this issue. Many Christian groups and leaders now do excellent work in seeking to broker peace. But overcoming our legacy of (and ongoing collusion in) religious intolerance towards Jews and Muslims remains a major obstacle to the potential for Christians to be trusted brokers.

Throughout history, and increasingly today, men and women of different faiths have found themselves on the Way of Blood, allowing religious difference to foment violent tribalism. We may be the victim of violence like the man in the parable or like Ali in the story that opened this chapter. But as Ali honestly acknowledges, we can be the aggressor too, and that includes Christians. We will now move on to explore how we have got to this point before returning to consider how we can be saved from the Way of Blood, saved from the religious tribalism that is tearing our world and our communities apart. That healing will stem from the insight that it may well be the religious other who comes to our aid. As Ali found in his encounter with Yitzhak, it may well be through the person of another faith that God is speaking and acting to redeem us.

Chapter 2

THINGS FALL APART

'I don't understand what is happening,' said the Cairo University professor. 'When I was a child my best friend was a Coptic Christian, and we used to tease and joke with each other about our religions. But now the young people are killing each other for their faiths. I do not understand what has happened.'

We met the professor on a day when some colleagues and I participated in an interfaith discussion between Muslims, Copts and Anglicans, hosted by the local bishop. Relations had been deteriorating between Christians and Muslims for some time, and senior religious leaders had invited us to facilitate some scriptural reasoning – thematic conversation around scriptural texts – among Cairo's younger religious scholars.

Tragically, on the day of our arrival a convoy of Coptic pilgrims 120 miles south of Cairo were intercepted by violent Islamists. Men were forced off the buses and ordered to recite the Shahada, the Muslim confession of faith. When they refused, the executions started, and by the end of the attack 28 people, including children, were dead. They added to a total of 100 Egyptians killed for being Christian in six months.

The professor we met shared the view of President Sisi that this was an invasion into Egypt by Islamist forces from another country, most likely Libya. But others we spoke to said that this violence would not be increasing in Egypt if there were not local hostility towards Christians. In any event, the Coptic participants in our scriptural reasoning session decided not to attend.

THE BREAKDOWN OF LIBERAL ORDER

The previous chapter opened up the issue of how we can engage with religious difference from a Christian perspective, and we saw how the Parable of the Good Samaritan might enable us to view religious difference as some kind of gift rather than a problem. We now take a step back to reflect on the context of our world today and to explore the confusion of the professor in this story. It is a confusion shared by many of us about what is happening that makes this need for interreligious understanding so urgent.

Religious violence seems to be on the increase everywhere, and there is no one victim and one oppressor.[1] As the story above illustrates, Christians are suffering at the hands of Muslims in Egypt. But Muslims are suffering at the hands of Buddhists in Myanmar and Jews in Palestine. Sikhs and Christians are suffering at the hands of Hindus in parts of India, and Hindus at the hands of Muslims in Kashmir. Atheists too, while continuing to suppress religions in China, are criminalised

---

1   The Pew Research Center's 2017 study on global restrictions on religion showed an increase in the percentage of countries with high or very high levels of social hostilities (i.e. acts of religious hostility by private individuals, organisations or groups in society) from 23 per cent to 27 per cent in 2015 (http://assets.pewresearch.org/wp-content/uploads/sites/11/2017/04/07161531/Pew-Research-Center-Religious-Restrictions-2017-FULL-REPORT.pdf).

in many countries, 13 of which punish atheism with death. And one of the challenges of our globalised, mobile societies is that these tensions spread around the world as diaspora communities, conscious of the suffering of their coreligionists in other parts are the world, are liable to project these tensions onto the different religious communities around them.

This is a problem we see at my university where two thirds of the students come from overseas. An atheist student from Iran may have experienced real persecution in their home country and want to use the greater freedom of their British university environment to campaign against this kind of oppression. But they need to remember that the British Muslim students against whom they may wish to direct that activism are themselves experiencing unprecedented levels of Islamophobia. When some students wore t-shirts at our student welcome fair displaying cartoons of the Prophet Muhammad, many within the university were quick to dismiss the Muslim students' complaints as oversensitivity in an environment that should be characterised by the promotion of free speech. But I was keen to remind people that new Muslim students were also arriving at this welcome event into a city of increased Islamophobic incidents and where that summer a mosque had been burned to the ground.[2]

This sort of unfair projection is now becoming commonplace as the kind of tribal identity that we explored in the last chapter becomes a part of many people's understanding of their citizenship in a globalised world. It is good, for example, that Western Christians have recently become more aware of the mass persecution of Christians in the Middle East. But projecting anger and fear about this situation onto

---

2   The Al-Rahma Islamic Centre in Muswell Hill was destroyed in a hate crime arson attack on 5 June 2013 in retaliation for the murder of a soldier in Woolwich the previous month.

the Muslims in our own communities is wrong and, in fact, counterproductive. Modelling a strong religious coexistence in our communities holds out the possibility of a better approach to religious difference in other parts of the world too. We feel this is particularly the case at the LSE where many students will go back to countries of intense religious conflict prepared, we hope, with skills for interfaith leadership.

So we need a better understanding of the causes of all this religious conflict. We need to better understand the reasons for this global spread of religious tribalism. That is a question that cannot be answered in isolation from the numerous forces that are shaping today's world: economic, social, political and ecological. Attempting to paint a comprehensive picture of these global trends in a book of this length is an almost ridiculous task. But it is important that religious issues are not just considered in isolation as if they operate entirely independently of other trends. Religious people are commonly inclined to do this. Take, for example, the issue of church attendance figures. If they go down, Christians tend to blame themselves (e.g. we are not welcoming enough, we are not evangelistic enough, etc.), and when they go up, they tend to attribute it to divine action (God has answered our prayers for more Christians). There may be truth in both these readings, but all of our actions, and presumably even those of God, take place within the broader pattern of history that has multiple ramifications for the question of whether people are more or less likely to attend church.

So this chapter will consider some of the broader trends that are affecting the religious landscape of today's world and address the very real feelings people have that we are currently going through a significant period of transition in global history. The argument of this chapter will be that the increased religious tribalism and conflict we are seeing is, in large part, a response to a broader crisis of the systems and ideas that have ordered the modern world. Every era has surely had its causes for concern and its prophets of doom. Just in the previous century, the upheavals of two world wars and the subsequent attempts to build a stable world order are ample reminder that human history is always turbulent. But what we appear to be experiencing today is the breakdown of many of the institutions and ideas that developed through the twentieth century and have dominated global governance and culture since the end of the Cold War. When Francis Fukuyama famously proclaimed the 'End of History' (Fukuyama 2012), he implied that the battle for ideas was over. With the collapse of the Soviet Union and the fall of the Berlin Wall, trans-national communism was defeated as a credible force. The model of the nation state gained universal dominance, and its purpose was to maintain the order of its societies through democratic representation, through participation in the market system and through the promotion of human rights. Implicit in the nation state model were certain secular assumptions, that all countries would follow a Western model of the relegation of religion to the private sphere. Any potential for religious tribalism was to be subordinated by a secular state.

The promotion of democracy, markets and human rights, underpinned by secular assumptions, was effectively the manifesto of globalisation as it developed through the last quarter of the twentieth century. Throughout the process there have been exceptional events that have bucked the trend towards liberal democracy, notably the Iranian revolution in 1979. But for a time the process seemed unstoppable and the optimism of the new era of globalisation was encapsulated in the 1989 inauguration address of President George H.W. Bush. Emboldened by the revolutions sweeping the Soviet Union that year, President Bush proclaimed that:

> a new breeze is blowing, and a world refreshed by freedom
> seems reborn. For in man's heart, if not in fact, the day of the

dictator is over. The totalitarian era is passing, its old ideas blown away like leaves from an ancient, lifeless tree. A new breeze is blowing, and a nation refreshed by freedom stands ready to push on.

Today it is hard to imagine any politician speaking with such optimism of the global landscape. Indeed, the key principles of this system – democracy, markets and human rights – are now all troubled and questioned concepts whose inevitable spread around the world can no longer be taken for granted. We will take a look at each of these in turn from both a domestic and then international perspective before coming on to consider the roles that religion and secularism play in these global changes.

Democracy

President Bush optimistically proclaimed that '[g]reat nations of the world are moving toward democracy through the door to freedom.' These former communist dictatorships were following the pattern of European colonies in the Global South that, through the twentieth century, had adopted the nation state model and democratic systems of their former imperial rulers. President Bush was heralding a new global order of freedom-loving nation states in which the democracy modelled in his own country would be a bulwark against tyranny. But 2016 saw the election of a very different President of the United States, one who has caused many people to raise questions about the health of democracy in this country that has propagated it around the world. Standing on a platform of populist criticisms of the political establishment, of out-of-control immigration and of a perceived disadvantage of American workers in the global economy, Donald Trump has confounded the naive perception that the 'will of the people' would always tend towards liberal values and rational discourse. What his election seemed to demonstrate was that large sections of the population had felt excluded from the mainstream political system. Their views were considered regressive or their experience of economic marginalisation was not taken seriously by a political class whom they considered to be an out-of-touch elite. But their champion was not one of their number, in the way the Labour movement of the twentieth century had raised up trade union leaders to transform a political system run by the upper classes. As David Goodhart suggests, the popular votes for both Trump and Brexit were motivated 'more by cultural loss, related to migration and ethnic change, than by economic calculation' (Goodhart 2017, p.2). Theirs was a popular champion for the media age, a television celebrity with the mass appeal of vast wealth, lavish promises and an intemperate rudeness that reassures his supporters that he is taking no prisoners in doggedly pursuing change on their behalf.

The paradoxes of this millionaire businessman turned hero of the dispossessed led former Archbishop of Canterbury Rowan Williams to argue that his election points to nothing short of 'the failure of mass democracy'. Politics has, he claims, 'been narrowed down to a mechanism for managing large-scale interests in response to explicit and implicit lobbying by fabulously well-resourced commercial and financial concerns' (Williams 2016). In other words, the scale at which democracy is seeking to operate in modern Western nations has become removed from the interests and experience of ordinary citizens and is, in effect, managed by greater powers (primarily corporate interests) from which they are disconnected. Politics, Williams argues, has to be an activity by which individuals and communities feel they are agents in the betterment of their own lives. For many today that feeling is lost. So in their impotence or frustration many are drawn to vote for iconoclastic and extreme figures who, in turn, will disappoint by failing genuinely to reconnect them with agency for change in their communities. Similar kinds of iconoclastic intentions were voiced during the Brexit debate, a desire to 'take back control' over our lives and our communities. So the success of Donald Trump and other right-wing figures in Europe, like Marine Le Pen in France or Nigel Farage in the UK, may well be a symptom of the fact that people no longer have confidence in democracy itself as a system. A recent poll showed that less than 30 per cent of British people in their 20s believe it is essential to live in a democracy. That compares with 70 per cent of people in their 80s (Foa and Mounk 2017).

If democracy is in crisis in the West, then we have increasing evidence to suggest that it is no longer the model to which the rest of the world aspires. In some regions there is the explicit rejection of the Western nation state model imposed at the end of the colonial era. That seems to be one feature of the Arab region today, the view among many that some sort of Islamic Caliphate might be a more authentically Arab model of governance rather than the Western-imposed democratic nation state.[3] In some of the world's major powers we are seeing theoretically democratic systems becoming taken over by authoritarian regimes who are eroding democratic freedoms, such as in Russia, Turkey and Egypt. And then of course it is worth remembering that 1.4 billion people live in China, an increasingly powerful regime that has never embraced democracy and has little apparent will to do so. That democracy is in crisis is well documented. The 2018 report *Freedom in the World* published by Freedom House,

---

3   This, for example, is the position of the pan-Islamist movement Hizb ut-Tahrir.

an American NGO supporting democracy, argued that 2017 saw the most serious undermining of democracy in decades. Seventy-one countries suffered a net decline in political rights and civil liberties while only 35 registered any gain. This was the twelfth consecutive year of overall erosion of democracy according to their measures. Its conclusions are stark:

> Democracy is in crisis. The values it embodies – particularly the right to choose leaders in free and fair elections, freedom of the press, and the rule of law – are under assault and in retreat globally. A quarter-century ago, at the end of the Cold War, it appeared that totalitarianism had at last been vanquished and liberal democracy had won the great ideological battle of the 20th century. Today, it is democracy that finds itself battered and weakened. (Freedom House 2018, p.1)

We must hope that democracy is not in terminal decline. Concern at recent political changes in Britain and America appears to be mobilising previously disengaged sections of society in the democratic process. According to an Ipsos MORI poll, youth turnout in the UK's 2017 General Election was the highest in 25 years, for example. But some serious dysfunctions have been exposed and democracy's inevitable spread can no longer be taken for granted.

Free markets

Returning to President Bush's inaugural address, the very next sentence links democracy with free markets, the fundamental driver of globalisation: 'Men and women of the world move toward free markets through the door to prosperity.' This has been the central tenet of Western economic thinking for the last 30 years. Powerful Western governments, supported by institutions like the IMF (International Monetary Fund) and

World Bank, insisted that participation in an unregulated market was the most effective route to growth. It was argued that government intervention in the market reduces competitive pressure by restricting the entry of competitors, whether through import controls or the creation of monopolies. This was economic orthodoxy from which few dared to stray.

The credibility of this view, however, has not recovered from the financial crisis of 2008 which gave ample evidence for the deficiencies of unregulated markets. Even though we have hardly shifted to a dramatically new model, the era in British economic thinking from Thatcher to Blair that presupposed the extension of markets and the rolling back of the state has come to an end. Calls for state rather than market control over key areas of the national infrastructure (such as the railways) no longer provoke the same level of ridicule that this amounts to regressive Marxist thinking. This kind of popular dissatisfaction with what is called the 'neo-liberal' economic system is clearly evidenced in the fact that the UK Brexit vote amounted to a decision to leave the largest and ostensibly most successful free trade block that the world has ever seen. Again, Rowan Williams's view of disempowerment and political alienation seems to provide some explanation here. Brexit and the rise of Trump and other anti-immigration politicians appear to be symptoms of many people's feeling that they are not well served by the way our society has been ordered under the free market. They may not verbalise it as a critique of neo-liberal economics but they know that simply voting for the other mainstream candidate will not be enough to bring back the jobs and community spirit that has been eroded in many former industrial communities.

The fact that immediate free trade has not been universally in the interests of developing nations has long been argued. History tells us that rich countries have always become rich, not through immediate participation in the free market, but through the use of protectionism and subsidies, which often continue after they have become rich! I remember encountering this when I worked for a junior member of the British government between 2001 and 2003. The UK was strongly endorsing GATS, the European Union's General Agreement on Trade in Services. This effectively compelled poor nations to privatise their public services and open them to foreign competition. But we were championing that policy while continuing to support the Common Agricultural Policy, which provided a €48 billion subsidy to European farmers that kept out imports from emerging economies. So while we preached free markets, in many sectors we continued to practise protectionism.

And concerns about the impact of unregulated markets have been borne out as a far greater level of inequality has been seen in those economies that have grown rapidly in recent years. Those include what were called the BRIC economies – Brazil, Russia, India and China. In 2012 the Brazilian economy overtook the UK as the sixth largest in the world. But that prosperity is far from equally shared: 20 per cent of the inhabitants of Rio de Janeiro live in *favelas*, the city's infamous slums. In 1950 that was only 7 per cent (see Davis 2006). India too is a country that has seen dramatic economic growth over the last couple of decades. But whereas 6 per cent of the nation's income went into the hands of the wealthiest 1 per cent of the population in the early 1980s, today this top 1 per cent captures 22 per cent of the income generated. This makes India the country with the widest gap in income distribution in the world today (Chancel and Piketty 2017). Market-based capitalism remains the unchallenged global economic system. But its limitations are felt in all corners of the world, and the political and social upheaval caused by its dysfunctions can no longer be ignored.

Human rights

The third building block of the Western vision is human rights, enshrined in the 1948 United Nations Universal Declaration. These are the ethical framework of democratic capitalism, and it had been assumed that any country embracing the first two values will inevitably adopt this third. Human rights are thought of in the Western liberal mind as some kind of inevitable discovery. The American Declaration of Independence a couple of centuries earlier put it that the equality and rights of all people were 'self-evident'. So it was assumed that the less human beings were held back by material need or lack of education, the more obvious and important these innate human rights would become. It was not self-evident, however, at the time of the Declaration of Independence that these rights extended to black people (to name but one anomaly). And still today, perhaps at an increased rate, we are seeing the implicit assumption that rights are *not* universal, that black lives or Muslim lives, or simply foreign lives don't matter as much as the lives of other citizens. It seems to many that while the theoretical language of human rights – universal, inalienable, indivisible – has spread around the world and been enshrined in treaties and charters, the reality has been rather different and such words have rung hollow, even in the Western countries who have championed them. Today, in response to the anxieties about migration discussed earlier, many countries are weakening their application of human rights to non-nationals. President Trump's ban on refugees from several majority-Muslim countries reneged on the Geneva Convention in its obligations to refugees. He has shown a similar disregard for the UN Convention Against Torture. But it is not only the United States. The British government has proposed replacing our Human Rights Act with a three-tiered Bill of Rights, with different levels of entitlement, something many human rights advocates consider to be a fundamental distortion of the very concept.

Other commentators argue that the Western human rights agenda has been essentially undermined by the methods Western governments have used to promote it. The spreading of human rights became a post-hoc justification for the 2003 invasion of Iraq, but the violent chaos that has engulfed the region for the many years since makes a mockery of the liberal hubris at work in such military interventions. Even longstanding trade relationships (particularly in armaments) can end up contributing to human rights abuses. So maybe self-evident human rights were always a bit of a fiction in the West. But the philosopher John Gray has argued that the greatest fiction was the inevitability of their spread under globalisation:

> There is no detectable connection between advancing globalisation and the spread of liberal values. Liberals resist this because it empties their lives of significance. For them liberalism is a surrogate religion, providing the sustaining illusion that their values express the meaning of history. (Gray 2016)

SHIFTING SECULAR ASSUMPTIONS

Clearly it would be an exaggeration to say that democracy, free markets and human rights are collapsing everywhere. Saudi Arabia, for example, has seen recent attempts to improve rights for women under Crown Prince Mohammad Bin Salman. But what John Gray points to is the demise of the idea that these concepts will inevitably define historical development. This is the view that history professor Timothy Snyder calls 'the politics of inevitability', a sense that the future is just more of the present, and that the laws of progress are known, that there are no alternatives, and therefore nothing really to be done' (Snyder 2018, p.7). The global dominance of the West is waning. Countries like China, Russia and India, which have different attitudes and alternative values system, are growing in size and economic and political power. We can no longer presume that the liberal democratic nation state model will be the one emerging states choose to adopt. Indeed, to many it felt like a colonial imposition. Far from universal and neutral in its origins, it was felt by many to be a legacy of the imperial age, native only to the American and European context.

The religious dimensions of this contemporary rejection are often neglected. This is primarily due to the extraordinary blindness that has developed in the Western world toward religion as a significant social and political force. We will explore this in the next chapter. But it is also due to the complex relationship that all three aspects of the liberal Western model that we have explored have in relation to religion, both in their origin and contemporary expression. On the one hand, they are ideas with religious (mostly Judaeo-Christian) roots. The development of democracy in the West owes a great deal to Christian thinkers such as John Calvin and even the earlier monastic tradition of electing abbots. Free markets, while now subject to strong Christian critique, chimed well in their early development with a global Christian vision of freedom and inclusion of all nations. Little wonder Adam Smith's claim that markets express the 'invisible hand of God' has resonated with so many. The human rights framework too, while now viewed by conservatives as conflicting with Christian social teaching, was largely codified by European Catholic thinkers. As Nick Spencer, thoughtful defender of Christianity's impact and legacy in Western culture, argues, 'at least until the 1960s, it was Christian-inspired or at least Christian-flavoured parties and movements that were responsible for the embedding of human rights within European and even global politics' (Spencer 2016, p.134).

But on the other hand, these ideas of democracy, free markets and human rights have mostly been emptied of their explicit religious content to form, as John Gray implies, a quasi-religious foundation for a secular society. So a new prominence of religion in public discourse and conflict can be seen as both cause and consequence of their weakening. As peoples around the world find this liberal world order less persuasive, so they turn increasingly to religious identities and religious social narratives. Far from seeing modern liberal values as grounded in (Christian) religion, they are more likely to associate them with a Western atheist society to which they no longer aspire.

Secularism was perhaps never explicitly stated as 'part of the package' in the Western liberal democratic model. America certainly retained a more explicitly religious identity than most European countries, while espousing a fairly uncompromising separation between church and state. But among most proponents of liberal order on both sides of the Atlantic, the received wisdom was that modernity's achievements had come about through the relegation and marginalisation of religion. In the European context this mythology stems back to the Wars of Religion in the sixteenth and seventeenth centuries and the view that the nation state emerged as the bulwark against religion's inevitable violence. The Treaties of Westphalia held the peace through the assumption that faith could be subordinate to citizenship and that transnational religious allegiances must not be allowed to threaten the state's sovereignty.

This political case for secularism as the precondition for a modern society chimes with a line of argument that has seen some revival in the face of secularism's recent crises. This is that the Enlightenment itself and all its achievements were not built on the platform of Europe's long and developed Christian tradition but won through religion's systematic defeat. Steven Pinker is one of the more recent champions of this view in his book

Enlightenment Now (Pinker 2018), which pushes back in support of all aspects of liberal order that he sees as arising from the Enlightenment and its victory over religious superstition. It is a robust defence of modernity, arguing essentially that our modern technological societies have 'never had it so good' and this is all down to the achievements of scientific, atheist humanism. But it strikes an implausibly Pollyannaish tone in a world where his optimism simply does not ring true with most people and his anti-religious sideswipes seem both defensive and naive. In a scrupulously fair review, Nick Spencer suggests that '[j]ust as he is wilfully blind about the Enlightenment's failings, he is wilfully blind about Christianity's positive contribution... Under no stretching of the imagination could the Enlightenment be imagined to be an atheist movement, for which Pinker is clearly straining to claim it' (Spencer 2018).

Unconvincing as the 'secularism = progress' thesis proves, it has been part of the mythology of the liberal order of Western modernity. The coupling of the spreading of democracy, free markets and human rights with secularism led to explicit attempts to marginalise religion from public life in the name of 'modernity'. Turkey is a particularly severe example where the nation state created by Kemal Atatürk after the fall of the Ottoman Empire sought dramatically to reduce the role religion played in society. Atatürk proclaimed that the Turkish people must:

> learn the principles of democracy, the dictates of truth and the teachings of science. Superstition must go. Let them worship as they will; every man can follow his own conscience, provided it does not interfere with sane reason or bid him against the liberty of his fellow-men. (quoted in Ellison 1928[4])

---

4   From a secondary source: *Atatürk: The Biography of the Founder of Modern Turkey* by Andrew Mango (1999): 'In a book published in 1928, Grace Ellison quotes [Atatürk], presumably in 1926–27'.

Thus Atatürk, in an effort to conform to a Western model, imported Western European ideas about the triumph of rationality over faith and the appropriateness of confining religion to a purely private dimension of life. Turkey is now going in a very different direction with its own inter-religious tensions.

Timothy Snyder argues that the modern, liberal *politics of inevitability* is giving way around the world to a *politics of eternity*. He uses this phrase primarily to indicate the way in which its champions (Donald Trump and Vladimir Putin are his primary examples) create an ahistorical narrative of crisis in which they offer protection to their citizens from external threats. 'Time is no longer a line into the future, but a circle that endlessly returns the same threats from the past… Progress gives way to doom' (Snyder 2018, p.8). But 'eternity' perhaps also points to a transcendent turn away from purely secular political theory. Snyder's analysis would benefit from greater consideration of the way in which religion is exploited, manipulated or even remedial in this new politics. In many countries moving away from liberal order, religion is a vehicle for emotional manipulation, renewed nationalist narratives and a force that unites people against perceived threats (tribalism). He does, in this regard, give an illuminating account of the spiritual power Putin has attained through his appropriation of the pseudo-Christianity of the fascist thinker Ivan Ilyin (1883–1954). As Communism took control of Russia in the early twentieth century, Ilyin distorted Christian ideas into a fascist politics designed to defeat Bolshevism. This involved the arrival of a redeemer figure who would be exempt from the Christian command to love in order to defeat Russia's enemies and lead Russia to salvation. He was exiled from Russia in 1922 but following the extraordinary rehabilitation of his ideas among Russia's post-Soviet elite, Putin arranged for his reburial in Moscow in 2005. This is but one illustration of how the crisis of liberal order has allowed for a recovery of religious thinking, both good and bad, as a new source of social identity and political philosophy. But it is to Egypt that we will now look for a more detailed case study of how the growth of religious conflict is connected to the collapse of liberal order.

BUILDING PARIS OR MECCA ON THE NILE

This chapter began with an encounter in Egypt that tells of confusion and alarm at a dramatic escalation in religious conflict. Egypt is a country with which the LSE Faith Centre has had some engagement, supporting dialogue between Muslims and Christians and links between the UK Foreign Office and the prestigious Al-Azhar Islamic University. It is a country of significant strategic importance in global interfaith relations, and I use it as a case study here as Westerners have become more and more aware of the religious instability of the country (particularly the increasing attacks on Coptic Christians)[5] while struggling to understand its complicated political developments, particularly since the Revolution of 2011. Geographically, Egypt is at the intersection of Africa, Europe and the Middle East, hence its historic importance for trade and travel via the Suez Canal. According to United Nations Development Programme statistics, demographically it is an enormous country of nearly 100 million of whom two thirds are under the age of 29. Religiously, it has played a key role, having an ancient Christian community that makes up 10 per cent of its population, being one of the first Arab

---

5   August 2013 saw a spike in church burnings across Egypt and several major terrorist attacks targeting Coptic Christians have been carried out in the years since, including the bombing of two Coptic churches in April 2017 and the killing of 28 pilgrims in Minya in May 2017, referred to at the start of the chapter.

countries to establish diplomatic relations with Israel, and rivalling Saudi Arabia in its leadership role across Sunni Islam through institutions of global reach like Al-Azhar University and the Muslim Brotherhood. The young population of this country will therefore have an important part to play in the fuelling or challenging of religious tribalism over the coming years. It is not my intention here to argue that the recent history of the country has been a straightforward reversion from Western liberalism to religious ideologies. Egypt's modern history has been a complex three-way struggle between nationalism, Islamism and differing visions of secular modernity, and that story stretches back well beyond the recent era of globalisation that we have sketched out since President Bush. But what we see today is a country in which the liberal order of Western-driven globalisation no longer seems a viable model and where bloody religious tribalism persists as a dominant and insoluble political force.

Egypt's liberal project began with Mohamed Ali's dynasty, under heavy colonial influence, in the first half of the twentieth century. The 1923 constitution saw a shift away from dynastic rule toward constitutional monarchy and an elected parliament. Democracy and civil freedoms were combined with a commitment to capitalist principles of private ownership, free trade and open markets. This was a time of great cultural openness to Europe. So impressed was Khedive Ismail Pasha after visiting Baron Haussmann's Parisian boulevards in 1867 that he sought to turn Cairo into a 'Paris along the Nile' and the aspiration to European cultural and intellectual life was felt well into the twentieth century. But these ideas remained alien to ordinary Egyptians, and it was the revolutionary programme brought in by Gamal Abdel Nasser when the monarchy was overthrown in 1952 that brought modernity to Egypt in a native form. Arab Nationalism turned away from America and the West and looked instead to Soviet

Russia for inspiration in addressing the economic inequality and class divisions that beset post-colonial Egypt. Nasser's policies were statist and socialist, so while he maintained an image of piety, making a well-publicised pilgrimage (*hajj*) to Mecca in 1954, he set himself against those who had an essentially Islamic vision for Egypt. These included the Muslim Brotherhood, an organisation founded by Hassan al-Banna in 1928 to promote political Islam and that had a large following on the streets. After a failed assassination attempt, Nasser arrested and tortured thousands of members of the Brotherhood suppressing their influence on Egyptian political life and ensuring the nominal secularity of Egypt under his rule. Nasser effectively nationalised religion, just like he brought other public goods into common ownership. Al-Azhar University was brought under the supervision of the Ministry of Religious Endowments, and he granted to himself the right to appoint the Grand Imam of Al-Azhar. It was not unlike Henry VIII's nationalisation of the Church of England!

Part of the popularity of Nasser's Arab Nationalism was his hostility to Israel and his identification of this Jewish nation as the common enemy of Arab states. Egypt's defeat in the Six Day War with Israel was, therefore, devastating to his credibility. More than that, it can be seen as a tipping point in the project of secularising Egypt and the wider Arab region. While the causes of this rapid defeat may well be purely military in terms of Egypt's over-commitment in Yemen and America's formidable resourcing of the Israeli army, Scott Hibbard argues that the conflict once again 'pitted a secular vision of society against the Islamist alternative' (Hibbard 2010, p.65). While leftists in the regime argued that the defeat pointed to failures fully to realise the modern society to which the revolution aspired, for the Muslim Brotherhood and other Islamists, the defeat was a direct result of Egypt's turning its back on God. Strong among the pious Muslim population was the view that:

the military officers' embrace of foreign ideologies – Marx was a German even if he was anti-capitalist – and their attempt to refashion Egyptian society on foreign models was their downfall. Despite its efforts to justify socialism along Islamic lines, the regime was nonetheless seen as un-Islamic and the establishment *ulema* [clerical leadership] as without credibility. (Hibbard 2010, p.66)

It was perhaps inevitable, therefore, that the regime of Nasser's successor, Anwar Sadat would move in a more overtly Islamic direction. While his inaugural speech affirmed his commitment to Nasser's legacy, he initiated a realignment in Egyptian politics that would marginalise the left-wing secular interests. Thousands of Brotherhood members imprisoned by Nasser were released from jail and their once outlawed newspaper *The Call* (*Al-Dawaa*) was again in circulation. The budget of Al-Azhar was dramatically increased giving Islamic scholars a greater platform in the state-controlled media. Apostasy laws were introduced, and Sharia law was declared the primary source for the Egyptian constitution. The wearing of the veil increased from 30 per cent to 64 per cent of Egyptian women in two decades, and Egyptian journalist Tarek Osman notes that the colloquial greetings between Egyptians on the street changed to the Islamic greeting 'peace be upon you' (*al-salamu aleikom*). Osman concludes, 'In less than a decade the civic nature of the Egyptian state of the 1950s and 1960s was replaced by a quasi-Islamic one; and a liberal public atmosphere and discourse became predominantly religious and conservative' (Osman 2013, p.30).

Charting this course from the open pro-European culture of the early twentieth century to the Islamist resurgence of the Sadat regime does not, of course, imply a linear drift away from the three elements of liberal Western order explored in this chapter of democracy, free markets and human rights. While Nasser's socialism emulated aspects of Western modernity,

Sadat's embrace of Islamism was in some ways designed to give cover to a more decisive openness to the West. Seeing the resolution of the Cold War, he effectively terminated the Soviet-leaning project of Arab Nationalism to ally himself squarely with the United States and broker a peace treaty with Israel. This meant a firm commitment to capitalism, the opening up of Egypt's markets and a shift away from the government, military and public sector towards the private sector. While harnessing the power of conservative Islam, Osman states that 'Sadat imagined *al-infitah* [his programme of political and economic reform] as laying the seeds for a democratic, capitalist, Western-oriented Egypt.' But, Osman goes on to argue that 'theory and practice did not converge' (Osman 2013, p.130). The main beneficiaries of Egypt's new liberalised economy were those close to the regime. Military and government elites benefited from a crony capitalism that had taken Nasser's wealth redistribution policies away from the poor but replaced them with little opportunity to participate in new prosperity. They saw little sign of increased democratic participation either as, for all his talk of Westernisation, Sadat's presidential power remained more in the absolutist mode of Egypt's ancient Pharaohs.

Anwar Sadat's assassination by Islamist militants in 1981 showed how untenable his marriage of political Islam with the Western state model proved to be; and if Egypt's years under the presidency of Hosni Mubarak can be defined by anything, it was an intensification of security at the expense of civil rights. Mubarak had witnessed Sadat's assassination in front of his own eyes, so while he maintained his predecessor's co-opting of conservative religious discourse in tension with his desire to be America's main Arab ally (particularly after the advent of the War on Terror), this fractious alliance could only be maintained through increased state repression. The state maintained its legitimacy in clamping down on the most extreme Islamists only by adopting much of the clothing of Islamism for itself. Those expressing dissenting views in politics or religion were attacked, commonly with the support of state institutions. Another consequence was the increased attacks on Egypt's Christian minority, which, while condemned by the hierarchy, seemed to be in line with the official assertion of Islam as the state religion. In short, argues Hibbard, '[i]nstead of providing a common basis of citizenship, the Mubarak regime's cynical bargain with Salafist Islam led to the political fragmentation of Egyptian society' (Hibbard 2010, p.94).

It was to celebrate the end of this repression and fragmentation that Egyptian students at the LSE organised a street party on our campus after Egypt's momentous, and largely peaceful, revolution in February 2011. They showed me pictures on their phones of their relatives at the demonstrations in Tahrir Square in Cairo. The 18 days of protests against President Mubarak's regime seemed to be led by the young, organised through new digital technology (a 'Facebook revolution') and championing precisely the Western ideals of democracy, a fairer economy and human rights. They seemed to want an inclusive, modern multifaith Egypt, and Muslim students at our street party asked to take a picture with me in my clerical collar to signify the healing of the conflicts between Muslims and Christians. They chanted the words that had echoed around Tahrir Square for the last 18 days: 'Raise your head high – you're Egyptian.' But we all joined in the party and shared in the optimism of the Arab Spring.

As we know, the eventual outcome of this revolution was, to most people, both surprising and disappointing in equal measure. Egypt held its first fully democratic elections in May 2012, and the Muslim Brotherhood candidate, Muhammad Morsi, won the ballot. A revolution to champion democracy and human rights and challenge crony capitalism seemed to result in the victory of a conservative Islamic movement perceived to be in contradiction with such Western values. By the summer of the following year Morsi was ousted by a military coup led by defence minister Abd al-Fattah al-Sisi who then assumed the presidency, much in the authoritarian mould of Mubarak. His leadership was confirmed in presidential elections in May 2014 after thousands of Muslim Brotherhood members had been imprisoned. What does this tell us about the state of democracy in Egypt today? For commentator H.A. Hellier, the events show the fragility of democratic ideals within a country habituated to autocratic leadership:

> Egypt had a democratic vote which the Muslim Brotherhood won, but Egypt was not a democracy. It was going through a democratic experiment... [W]hile Morsi had the mandate to be president, it was all predicated on the success of the democratic experiment itself. (Hellier 2016, p.97)

This reasoning is what enables many progressive-minded Egyptians to accept President Sisi's reassertion of military power over the Muslim Brotherhood, even if this contradiction of the ideals of the revolution is a hard pill to swallow. No one can argue that democracy exists in Egypt today.

What of free market capitalism? LSE academic Armine Ishkanian links the malfunctioning of democracy in Egypt with the malfunctioning of economic policies. She sees the 2011 revolution as the culmination of a series of civil protests at increased poverty and inequality that were progressively brought about by the implementation of free market economics (Ishkanian and Glasius 2018). She argues that Sadat's *infitah* policies were compounded by successive waves of economic restructuring, directed by the IMF, liberalising trade and privatising public assets in a manner that consolidated wealth in the ruling elite. The revolution cannot, therefore, be separated from the 2008 financial crisis, which pushed up food prices and exacerbated resentment. If the revolution was a cry for democracy, it was prompted by a failure of free markets.

And human rights? In February 2018 the BBC journalist Orla Guerin undertook a harrowing investigation into the dramatic increase in enforced disappearances in Egypt (Guerin 2018). The Egyptian Commission for Rights and Freedoms has documented at least 1,500 enforced disappearances in the past four years. The issue was particularly brought to European attention by the abduction, torture and murder of an Italian PhD student from Cambridge University, Giulio Regeni, who had been researching trade union movements in Cairo. But, of course, the vast majority of those who disappear are local Egyptians, most of whom are accused of opposing the current regime or threatening it in some way. Many are Islamists or supporters of the Muslim Brotherhood, who are subsequently charged with terrorist offences, but campaigners contest the charge that many pose a violent threat. But the victims of human rights abuse are not just the Islamists and those who might resent the deposition of President Morsi. Also among those in detention are figureheads of the 2011 revolution. Guerin tells the story of Alaa Abdel Fattah. An icon of the revolution, 36-year-old Alaa represented Egypt's progressive generation – charismatic, secular, a blogger and software developer. Now Alaa is behind bars, charged with organising a protest against the use of military courts in civilian trials. Virtually all forms of protest in Egypt have now been banned, a deterioration even from the Mubarak regime.

The story of Egypt has been told here, not to single out a particularly tragic case of recent political crisis, but as a salient illustration of broader global trends within a country of major strategic importance in East–West and interreligious relations. Over the course of a century, Western ideas and values –

particularly those of democracy, free markets and human rights – have sought to shape Egyptian society but have ultimately been found wanting in different ways. Democratic processes have been frustrated and overturned as the culture of democracy has not taken root. Free markets have not created the shared economic prosperity that they promised. And human rights have been progressively eroded as central authority has imposed an ever-tighter grip on dissenting political views. With their erosion has gone the erosion of secular principles. These include both the principle of some state separation from religion (government control over Al-Azhar and the regulation of imams remains as strong as ever) and the attempt to confine religion to the merely private sphere of life. Even with suppression of the Muslim Brotherhood it is no longer possible to think that Islamist ideas can be removed from popular political discourse in Egypt and the tension between religious identities (particularly Muslim/Christian) constitutes a primary fault line in Egyptian society.

I want to argue that the breakdown of Western liberal order is both cause and effect of this resurgent religious discourse and identity. Religion as a primary social force had never gone away. But the secular assumptions of the Western worldview had led many to play down its significance or assume its inexorable decline. As the foundations of this Western worldview have been shaken, so religion has re-emerged and simultaneously, as in the case of Egypt, become the primary vehicle for the challenging of these Western principles.

THE END OF LIBERAL ORDER IN THE WEST

Egypt has been our example of the ways in which Western-led globalisation is being rejected in the non-Western world. But as we noted earlier in this chapter, the foundations of liberal order are in crisis in our own countries too. We also have less confidence in democracy, free markets and human rights to bring about the kind of societies we want to live in. In a curious way, while our societies have continued to secularise (we look at this in more detail in the next chapter), this has also meant that the ghosts of the religious imagination have come back to haunt us. As our quasi-religious framework of liberal modernity has been shaken, its religious antecedents are once again in the air, either as nightmarish visions of the pre-modern irrationalism into which we might collapse, or as nostalgic visions of a lost Eden, a time when we had purpose, community and a transcendent social goal.

The former is well expressed in Michel Houellebecq's 2015 novel *Submission*. The novel is set in France, a nation associated with some of the strongest understandings of secular principles within the public sphere. *Laicité* is interpreted as the exclusion of religious language and symbols from public institutions and is seen as a fundamental principle of French citizenship. So Houellebecq imagines an almost dystopian scenario where the charismatic leader of the French wing of the Muslim Brotherhood forms an alliance with the socialists to become the successful candidate in the 2022 presidential election against the far-right candidate Marine le Pen. Islamic law is enforced, women wear the veil and polygamy is encouraged. All of this is particularly seen through the prism of the university, a symbol of French enlightenment and equality. The story's narrator, a university lecturer named François (the name means Frenchman) seems himself to represent a decadent French society: he is tired, ill, socially isolated and profoundly depressed. He suffers from that most French of diseases, ennui. Ultimately François too 'submits' to Islam, not with passion and fervour, but pragmatism and resignation that the *ancien régime* is no more.

It is a novel shot-through with stereotypes about Islam, particularly in relation to women ('Muslim women were devoted and submissive…they aim to please' (p.247)), and colludes with paranoid fantasies of cultural takeover in a manner reminiscent of twentieth-century fears about Jewish conspiracies.[6] But the story is fundamentally about the failures of the modern story that France has been telling about itself. The plot plays on the crisis of democracy that has seen the once marginal *Front National* become a major player in a polarised political scene that mirrors the state of many contemporary democracies. Its laboured depiction of an assault on women's rights reveals a profound anxiety that the French Republic's principle of *egalité* is ultimately precarious. And behind its ideas is much cultural Marxist theory that globalised capitalism has significantly diminished a state once defined by a powerful public sector, particularly in relation to education.

But if Houellebecq's novel reflects fears about a future lapse into religiosity, it also contains nostalgic sentiments about Europe's Christian past. François is a scholar of Joris-Karl Huysmans, a nineteenth-century French novelist who found his own response to decadence and nihilism in a conversion to Roman Catholicism. In a central section of Houellebecq's novel, François travels to Rocamadour to see the Black Virgin, one of the most important religious icons of the Middle Ages. Alone and lost, he is drawn to the statue:

> Every day I went and sat for a few minutes before the Black Virgin – the same one who for a thousand years inspired so many pilgrimages, before whom so many saints and kings had knelt. It was a strange statue. It bore witness to a vanished universe. (Houellebecq 2015, p.135)

---

6   I am thinking particularly here of *The Protocols of the Elders of Zion* (c.1902), a fabricated anti-Semitic text purporting to describe a Jewish conspiracy for global domination.

If François is unable to connect spiritually with this tradition in the manner of his hero Huysmans, this gives us a glimpse of a religious nostalgia that is another feature of our contemporary situation in Western society. From an evangelical ascendancy that sees the Bible as a firmer foundation for society than modern liberal order, to a dramatic growth in those drawn to the ethereal worship of English cathedrals (see Jenkins 2016), there are signs in our culture too of the mourning for a perceived religious past and, in some cases, the desire to re-establish it.

Western society in late modernity is sometimes thought to be defined by the 'death of God'. We have sought to establish our societies and their values (not least democracy and human rights) on religionless principles. Yet, the late French philosopher Jean Baudrillard once wrote that 'God has departed, but he has left his judgement behind, the way the Cheshire Cat left his grin' (Baudrillard 2003, p.4). Perhaps Houellebecq's book, and the broader persistence of religion in our culture, expresses an enduring judgment that the way we have organised our society is not what it might be. Our values and vision lack the potency of the religious imaginations that formed our past and that many in today's world are identifying as the means of imagining a better future. As we have seen, this religious reaction to political crisis is often extremely disturbing, such as in the pseudo-Christian fascism Timothy Snyder detects in Russia or the intolerant Islamism that threatens the future of Coptic Christians in Egypt. Other religious elements in this response can be seen more positively as the renewal of identity and moral purpose in a world that has become atomised and de-moralised by market logic and individualist thinking. Debates about the virtue or otherwise of religion in the public sphere can surely only intensify. As the central pillars of our liberal world order – democracy, free markets and human rights – continue to show their inadequacy in the face of today's challenges, it seems that more of the Cheshire cat's face is reappearing. And this is what we will explore in our next chapter.

Chapter 3

THE RETURN
OF RELIGION

We had spent two hours with LSE students of different faiths talking about three scriptural texts, one from the Hebrew Bible, one from the New Testament, and one from the Qur'an. We had shared our own interpretations, discussed common themes, and received the fresh perspectives of those reading our familiar texts with outsiders' eyes. At the end of the session I asked each student to share with the group one new thing they had learnt. A Jewish student said, 'When I was a kid, I turned on the Discovery Channel and saw this man being tortured on a cross. I thought it was really disturbing and that Christianity was weird. But today I've learned some of the things Jesus said. He was pretty cool.' A Christian student remarked, 'I never knew that Islam gave such a privileged place to Jews and Christians as "People of the Book". I've learned that Muslims have a far higher view of Christians than Christians tend to have of them.' A Baha'i student added, 'I never knew that I could learn so much from fellow students about religion. We come here from all around the world, and we're all so diverse. But this is a secular university, and you don't feel you can talk about religion. I'm really glad we have today.'

SECULARISM IN RETREAT

Some readers of this book may be struggling to find the overall thesis entirely plausible. The idea that secularism has withered on the vine and that religious narratives will define the coming century may seem rather remote to many readers' day-to-day experience. This is because we in the Western world live with a great paradox. Essentially, the Western experience of secularisation is continuing (perhaps even accelerating) while, globally, a strong case can be made that secularism is in retreat. In 2016 I was invited to speak to a group of students in an Anglican secondary school in Western Australia. Prior to the class I had preached for the School Founders Day service in a magnificent neo-Gothic chapel. Hundreds of smartly dressed boys and teachers in academic gowns packed in for a vibrant liturgy with lusty hymn singing and a celebration of the Eucharist in which the majority of staff and students received communion. But when I began my class I asked the students to put up their hand if they thought religion was dying out in the world today. Every boy in the room put up his hand. Australia is one of the most rapidly secularising countries in the world with those affiliating to no religion expected to rise to over 40 per cent by 2050.[1] That increase will come almost entirely from traditional Christian denominations who are haemorrhaging members, particularly among the age group of these students. So even for these young people for whom the practice of faith is part of their daily lives, religion seems increasingly anachronistic, irrelevant and in terminal decline.

Much of the UK is experiencing a similar disconnection from the Christian past. The 2011–2012 British Social

---

1   Pew-Templeton Global Religious Futures Project: www.global religiousfutures.org/countries/australia#/?affiliations_religion _id=0&affiliations_year=2050&region_name=All%20Countries &restrictions_year=2015

Attitudes Survey showed that religious affiliation in Britain continues to decline, and rapidly. Fifty per cent of people are now classified as 'nones' (affiliating to no religion) and that rises to 70 per cent when you look at young people aged 18–25.[2] The Church of England has become almost a byword for decline, losing members of its congregations year-on-year since the Second World War and with discouraging projections for at least the next 20 years. Nearly a third of regular Anglican church attenders are over 70.[3]

The Church of England has a vast parochial network of stunning churches, many in places that are unlikely to see dramatic revival. So, like the Australian schoolboys, even those of us for whom religion is part of daily life may find it difficult to identify with the idea that the twenty-first century belongs to religion.

One exception to this trend, however, has been London, where, from the early 1990s, the Anglican diocese saw a 20-year period of steady growth.[4] Numerous factors have been identified in this bucking of the trend. There has been an opening up of the traditional parochial model to allow church plants and new worshipping communities, which attract those alienated from traditional forms of church. Several 'powerhouses' of growth have developed with big resources and high production values to attract large gathered congregations, which have themselves then planted churches in their style. Effectively, in a city where parish boundaries make little sense to a new 'networked' generation, a more

---

2   See Chapter 12: Losing Faith?, pp.173–184 in Park *et al.* (2012).

3   *Statistics for Mission 2016*, Church of England Research and Statistics 2017: www.churchofengland.org/sites/default/files/2017-10/2016 statisticsformission.pdf

4   See *A Capital Idea* (2003) and *Another Capital Idea* (2011), reports of the Diocese of London: www.london.anglican.org/about/another-capital-idea

fluid entrepreneurial model has been adopted to meet diverse tastes and erratic lifestyles.

But, without doubt, the principal factor in London's religious revival has been its status as a 'world city', a global intersection where the secularising West intermingles with a world of religious resurgence. As many as 39 per cent of the citizens of central London were born overseas. The top five countries that these Londoners come from are India, Poland, Pakistan, Nigeria and Romania. All of these countries are seeing forms of religious resurgence made possible by the trends discussed in the last chapter. So in the 2011 census London had the highest proportion of non-Christian religions of any UK region and the lowest growth among the 'nones'.[5] Sociologist Tariq Modood describes how London has shifted from being the godless capital of a broadly Christian nation to being the religious centre of an otherwise secular country (Modood and Calhoun 2015, p.8). We might say that London is becoming a 'post-secular' city, and this was vividly illustrated at the swearing-in ceremony in 2016 of London's first Muslim mayor (one of a million Muslims now living in London). This ceremony took place, not at City Hall or some other civic building, but at Southwark Cathedral in a ceremony at which the new mayor was flanked by bishops, rabbis, imams and leaders of numerous other faith communities. It is hard to imagine this kind of civic event, characterised by diverse religious inclusion, taking place in London just 20 years ago.

That image of Sadiq Khan's swearing-in ceremony, set in the context of growth in London's Christian denominations, challenges a strongly held perception of a 'zero-sum game' in the current global religious resurgence. Many people are

---

5   See the Office of National Statistics website for full details www.ons. gov.uk/peoplepopulationandcommunity/culturalidentity/religion/ articles/religioninenglandandwales2011/2012-12-11

persuaded by Michel Houellebecq's fears discussed in the last chapter, believing that if secularism is declining in the UK it is only because Islam is growing and that this constitutes a fundamental threat to Christian identity and even to national security. In February 2018 the Prime Minister of Hungary, Viktor Orbán, used his state of the nation address to say that migration had 'opened the way to the decline of Christian culture and the expansion of Islam'. He argued that 'Islamic civilisation – which has always seen its mission as the conversion of Europe to what it calls the true faith – will knock on Central Europe's door not only from the South, but also from the West.'[6] This allusion to a recurrent external threat from which only defiant leadership can protect its citizens certainly puts him into the camp of Timothy Snyder's 'politics of eternity'. In reality, the 2011 census showed that the Muslim proportion of Hungary amounts to little more that 0.1 per cent of the population.

This anxiety about a shift from Christianity to Islam is often the elephant in the room in intra-Christian conversations including the ongoing controversies of the global Anglican Communion. We have seen dramatic shifts in the demographics of Anglicanism, which have brought the politics of interreligious conflict to the fore in our intra-Anglican conflicts. In 1900 more than 80 per cent of Anglicans lived in Britain and a mere 1 per cent lived in sub-Saharan Africa. By 2008 the critical mass of Anglicanism had shifted to the global south with 55 per cent of Anglicans living in sub-Saharan Africa, and that percentage will have grown significantly in the past decade. Sub-Saharan Africa is beset with problems

---

6   Viktor Orbán's state of the nation address can be read in full on the Hungarian government website: www.kormany.hu/en/the-prime-minister/the-prime-minister-s-speeches/viktor-orban-s-state-of-the-nation-address

of interreligious conflict, and many Christians are in mortal danger from Islamist militant groups, such as Boko Haram in Nigeria and the Islamist Al-Ingaz regime in South Sudan. Paranoia about an Islamification of many parts of the world is widespread. At a gathering of new bishops from around the Anglican Communion a Nigerian bishop took me aside and played the video of a news report on his phone that contrasted declining Anglican churches with overflowing mosques and predicted the full 'Islamification' of Britain in the next decade. I reassured the bishop that while the Church of England had no cause for complacency, the last census put the Muslim population at 4.4 per cent compared to the Christian 60 per cent and that our relations with the minority Muslim community were mercifully far more cordial than his own situation in Nigeria. The point is that many people, in Western nations and around the world, are experiencing the spread of religious pluralism brought on us by mass migration and technological change as an existential threat, and that is leading to religious tribalism.

But for all people's anxieties (particularly that of Western Christians) about the growth of the religious other, the reality is that, when you look at the global data, *all* the world religions (with the exception of Buddhism) are growing numerically.[7] Christianity is expected to reach nearly three billion followers by 2050 retaining its proportion of 31 per cent of the global population. Our Western experience of secularisation has not been replicated in the rest of the world (see also Davie 2002). The Australian schoolboys were all wrong. Religion is not dying. It is growing.

---

7   Pew Research Center, *The Future of World Religions: Population Growth Projections 2010–2015*, www.pewforum.org/2015/04/02/religious-projections-2010-2050. Buddhism's decline is attributable to low fertility rates and ageing populations in countries such as China, Thailand and Japan.

The former Chief Rabbi Jonathan Sacks puts it succinctly: 'The seventeenth century was the dawn of an age of secularization. The twenty-first century will be the start of an age of desecularization' (Sacks 2015, p.18). The last chapter set the scene for explaining this desecularisation. The globalisation of key Western ideas with their secular assumptions is floundering. We are seeing crises in some core political, social and economic ideas, and religion is both a cause and effect of this. The obvious example is the way in which Islam has become a post-colonial political force, particularly in the Arab region. In his analysis of the rise of ISIS, Professor Fawaz Gerges describes how so much of the political and social infrastructure of the Middle East has simply broken down (Gerges 2017). Democracy, capitalism, human rights and many other elements of a functioning society are not working, and political Islam is one of the ideologies filling the void. As the liberal democratic nation state model, imposed by former colonial powers, has disintegrated, we can see why ideas from Muslim history, such as the caliphates of the medieval period, fire the imagination of many for a better future.

Needless to say, the so-called Islamic Caliphate that has dominated the struggles of the Levant region in recent years is a million miles from the historical realities of the Umayyad, Abbasid and Ottoman Caliphates, which offer us some of the best examples in history of religious pluralism and scientific advancement. But while Islam dominates the headlines, we could also look at numerous examples from across the faith traditions where political or economic frustrations are finding a religious mode of expression, often fused with forms of nationalism. We could look at the Hindu nationalism that is now dominating Indian politics and has led leading politicians in the ruling BJP (Bharatiya Janata Party – the 'Indian People's Party') to declare that India, a country that has lived for centuries with radical religious pluralism, is officially Hindu in a parallel manner to how Pakistan is described as Islamic. Or we could look at the way in which religious ideas are now dominating Israeli politics to an extent never conceived by the early Zionists. Just as Prime Minister Nerandra Modi uses overt Hindu rhetoric to strengthen his government in India, Benjamin Netanyahu of Israel does not shy away from appealing to the Bible to support his claims, such as that Jerusalem should be recognised as the 'eternal' capital of Israel by other countries. President Trump, of course, uses the same strategy, appealing directly to Christian voters in America with biblical texts and public prayers. So we are seeing a strengthening of religious identity politics across the faith traditions and across the world in a way that is leading, in some places, to increased religious affiliation and increased religious observance.

In addition to religion becoming the new vehicle for political concerns, there are two important factors to consider in understanding this return of religion. The first may appear slightly at odds with the arguments of the last chapter, which saw the failures of Western-led globalisation as a cause of secularism's weakened appeal. Globalisation has also *spread* religion, and a major factor in the global growth of religious affiliation has been the end of the Cold War and the defeat of Communism. Take the example of Russia. Here is a country where atheism was enforced for most of the twentieth century but which has now seen an extraordinary revival of the Orthodox Church. Those without religious affiliation have dropped to a mere 15 per cent of the population,[8] and it would seem that much of the cultural sense of belonging that

---

8   See Pew Research Center analysis, *Religious Belief and National Belonging in Central and Eastern Europe*, May 2017: www.pewforum. org/2017/05/10/religious-belief-and-national-belonging-in-central -and-eastern-europe

had been supplied by membership of the Communist party and its institutions has been transferred to the Church.[9] Russia is one of a number of former communist countries where, as we saw earlier, a brand of religious nationalism has been part of the forging of a new identity and a new national pride. China is another interesting example. This is a country of 1.4 billion where data on religious affiliation is difficult to obtain, but we know that it is growing dramatically. There are now more Christians in Church on Sunday in China than in the whole of Europe.[10]

It was only to be expected that the failures, and collapse, of the atheist system of Communism in much of the world would lead to a resurgence of religion. Global capitalism has even propagated forms of religion conducive to capitalist development. I sometimes talk to Chinese students who are drawn to learning more about Christianity because they associate it with Western development and consumer capitalism, something that feels a long way from the reality of Jesus' life and his teaching on the virtue of poverty! This is essentially the argument of former editor of *The Economist* John Micklethwaite in his book *God is Back: How the Global Rise of Faith Will Change the World* (Micklethwaite and Wooldridge 2009). In its millennium edition *The Economist* newspaper had printed God's obituary. So this book is a form of recantation, acknowledging that the secularist assumptions held by their publication, along with most Western European journalists

---

9   It is interesting to note that while affiliation to the Russian Orthodox Church rose from 31 per cent to 72 per cent of the population in the period 1991–2008, Pew Research Center suggest that this has not resulted in a similar increase in church attendance, suggesting precisely this politicisation of religious identity. See www.pewforum. org/2014/02/10/russians-return-to-religion-but-not-to-church

10 Based on the Chinese government's own figures reported by the BBC (see Gardam 2011).

and commentators, had proved ill-founded. Micklethwaite and his co-author Adrian Wooldridge particularly focus on the Pentecostal Christianity that has grown dramatically around the world, which often preaches a kind of prosperity gospel (earn God's favour and God will reward you materially) that appeals to those seeking a better life for themselves and their families. The prolific Pentecostal churches that can often spring up overnight on urban streets around the world frequently provide miraculous healing ministries that are a consolation to people deprived of expensive healthcare. So perhaps we can say that on the one hand the spread of free market capitalism has led to the growth in certain kinds of religion. But on the other hand, religious affiliation is also fuelled by the failure of Western consumer capitalism to deliver on its promises.

The other crucial cause of global desecularisation is simple demographics. The least religious parts of the world are having fewer children than the most religious parts. Birth rates in Europe have long been far lower than more devout corners of the world such as sub-Saharan Africa. The reality is that, when you look at the global data, the impact of believers changing their faith or leaving their faith is very minimal. The vast majority of new adherents to any faith tradition (or non-faith tradition) are simply born, and growth is primarily a matter of birth rates. So this is where data provided by the Pew Research Center in Washington DC gives the strongest support to the desecularisation thesis. Their projections suggest that the proportion of the world that is not religious will shrink from 17 per cent today to 13 per cent by 2050,[11] and that is in spite of dramatic growth in disaffiliation we have recently seen in the United States, which had long bucked the European secularisation trend. So it is an incredibly complex

---

11 Pew Research Center, *The Future of World Religions: Population Growth Projections 2010–2015*, www.pewforum.org/2015/04/02/religious-projections-2010-2050

picture with many variables that are hard to predict. But for all the reasons set out above, religion is again a highly potent force in the world. It is not going away; it is growing.

The temptation for those of us who are religious is to become triumphalist at this fact. Many of us grew up in a culture with the ingrained perception that religious observance was odd and marginal. I was the only child in my primary school class who regularly attended church. I remember feeling that my peers saw religious commitment as noble but eccentric, and there were certainly, in their view, many more fun things you could do on a Sunday morning. It feels to me that the culture is changing and that perhaps the growing awareness that we live in a multifaith society is making people more conscious of how religion plays a major part in more people's lives than we used to recognise. British young people are now growing up with an understanding that religion is one strand of identity politics and, at least in theory therefore, to be respected. But it is also said that these days we are prone to living in 'echo-chambers' that reinforce our views. Social media feeds us ideas and opinions that reflect our pre-existing tastes. So it is still alarmingly common to find people with a rigid and myopic view about religion (be that a religious or a non-religious view) that they are highly resistant to having challenged. It continues to surprise me how many people are still shocked that the London School of Economics should have a centre dedicated to religious provision and engagement. But when you look at the makeup of the student body (two thirds from overseas and almost 60 per cent from outside of Europe) it really should be no surprise.

The fact that secularist and atheist assumptions are no longer the defining narrative may rightly renew hope and confidence among those of us who believe that the flourishing of humanity is related to the discernment of God's purposes for the world. But triumphalism is misplaced, because we cannot say that more religion is *per se* a good thing. Many of the dominant forms of religion in today's world are violent and sectarian. Many are unsophisticated in their interpretation of scripture and set themselves in opposition to an enlightened appreciation of scientific discovery. Many are divisive and exclusive rather than generous and reconciling. So we cannot be pleased that there is simply more religion around. As Bishop Tom Wright once remarked to those inclined to Christian triumphalism, 'We live in a very religious age. But this has little to do with Jesus or Christianity. Jesus and his first followers lived in a very religious age. Look what it did to them' (Wright 1999, p.65). In many ways a better understanding of the nature of appropriate secularity and the kinds of institutions we need to promote religious and non-religious pluralism should be of major concern to today's conscientious believer as much as the promotion of a singular faith perspective.

The next chapter will explore some specifically Christian thinking on the kinds of institutions and social attitudes needed to build a healthy pluralism. But the remainder of this chapter will focus on how society more broadly needs to adjust in order to take on board these largely unexpected considerations of religious diversity, religious resurgence and religious conflict in today's world. I will argue that our response needs to be twofold. First, we need to learn and, second, we need to act.

RELIGIOUS LITERACY: ENGAGING THE IMAGINATION

The phrase 'religious literacy' would probably have sounded rather odd to most people at the end of the last century. The term 'literacy' has slowly come to denote competence in a range of areas: digital literacy, media literacy, and so on. Religious literacy is a recent addition as this phrase has become the vehicle for the argument that a good level of knowledge about world religions is a necessary component in global citizenship. This is true within general education. The UK Commission on Religious Education agreed with the premise of this chapter in stating, 'Young people are growing up in an ever more complex world where religious and non-religious worldviews are increasingly influential. Religious education (RE) has a distinctive contribution to make in equipping them for adult life and citizenship in this environment.'[12] Part of the 'religious literacy revolution' has been a moving away from the notion that learning about religion is necessarily a purely confessional activity (like learning Bible stories in Sunday school) to thinking of it as the gaining of important, more general understanding about widely held beliefs, which you may or may not hold yourself. France's secularist approach has traditionally conceived that religious education could only be the former, a catechetical faith formation that does not belong in state-funded education. Britain has taken a more open view, long requiring the teaching of a range of faiths. But the significant role that local religious leaders play on the statutory Standing Advisory Councils for Religious Education (SACREs), which set the RE curriculum and oversee collective worship in schools, suggests that we are still wedded to the notion that there is some confessional element to this learning (we don't have a council of Spanish people to oversee the teaching of Spanish in British schools). But the general trend has been towards a broad education in religious ideas and practices in which the faith stance of the learner is a secondary issue. Even in France, recent Muslim-related terrorist incidents such as the mass killings in the Bataclan

---

12 The Very Reverend Dr John Hall in the foreword to *Religious Education for All*, Interim Report of the Commission on Religious Education (2017).

nightclub have resulted in tentative steps to incorporate some religious literacy within the French school curriculum.

Religious literacy is not just a matter for schools, however. Different professional sectors are identifying the particular kinds of religious literacy their workers need to do their jobs more effectively and to facilitate better relationships in the working environment. Multinational corporations, for example, may need to train staff about the religious customs that will be practised by colleagues and clients in different countries around the world. A whole industry is emerging to meet these different needs, and the LSE Faith Centre has been involved in providing religious literacy training for British diplomats. Diplomats, too, need to learn about the customs and sensitivities particular to different faiths, such as not eating and drinking in Ramadan or not turning your back to a statue of the Buddha. They may meet religious leaders and need to understand their position and beliefs. But, more than that, given the prominence of religion in the politics of today's world they need a sophisticated level of religious literacy to engage with religious communities at a deeper level. That may be in the combating of violent religious extremism and the countering of theological arguments that would deny people the right to freedom of religious expression. Or it may be harnessing the strong social capital of religious communities in overcoming disease or poverty.

So this raises the question of the kind of religious literacy that is of genuine use in today's world. It is clearly important to learn the basic tenets of the main world faith traditions. We should be familiar with the five pillars of Islam and the story of Guru Nanak. But once we've learned those things, how far has that got us? What kind of literacy have we really obtained and what difference does it make to our engagement in a world of religious diversity and conflict? It is another liberal shibboleth that learning is always a positive thing and always benefits both the individual and society. But we should not reject the possibility that increased religious knowledge could feed a more sophisticated hatred. Michel Houellebecq is not ignorant about Islam, but his book (discussed in the last chapter) has not furthered the cause of interreligious harmony.

Religious literacy is not just sets of information and facts. As we have sought to make students more religiously literate, my colleagues and I have come to the view that it is more like the building of a skill set that enables people to navigate the languages, symbols and practices of different religious traditions and to develop some sense of empathy with their adherents. Our argument is that the presence of resurgent religion in the world today requires both learning and action, or rather *a learning that enables us to act effectively* in being better citizens, in engaging constructively with difference, and in receiving the wisdom that can be shared within a religiously plural world. Central to our understanding of this kind of learning is an entering into the world's multiple religious imaginations. Improving our understanding of those who hold different religious or non-religious views to ourselves will not simply be a matter of gaining knowledge so much as a shift in imagination. In the religious literacy programmes that we run at LSE we are concerned that students don't just learn what other people believe but rather *how different religious believers imagine the world and their place within it.* Imagination is important in everyone's worldview. No one sees the world purely empirically; we all hold beliefs, assumptions and ideals that frame our interactions with others and our shared quest for meaning. Religious imagination is the particular moral and cultural universe within which a religious believer thinks and acts. Imagination is also crucial in defining the world that we are all working towards. What do we hope for? What kind of vision do we have for the justice and peace of the world? How do we seek to better ourselves and contribute to society?

All of these are things that we imagine in order to bring about. In the Western world, we overlook the predominance of religious narratives in this kind of imaginative framing and forget how much religion has shaped our own imagination.

A book that we have found useful in thinking about religious imagination as we have established our programmes at the LSE Faith Centre is Jonathan Haidt's *The Righteous Mind: Why Good People are Divided by Politics and Religion* (Haidt 2012).[13] Haidt is a social psychologist who explores moral decision-making. His basic thesis is that ethical reasoning is always secondary to our moral intuitions (we do what *feels* right and then we theorise the decision later). He identifies five foundations of moral intuition. The first is the Care/Harm foundation. This evolved in response to the adaptive challenge of caring for vulnerable children. It makes us sensitive to signs of suffering and need; it makes us despise cruelty and want to care for those who are suffering. The second is the Fairness/Cheating foundation. This evolved in response to the adaptive challenge of reaping the rewards of cooperation without getting exploited. It makes us sensitive to indications that another person is likely to be a good (or bad) partner for collaboration and reciprocal altruism. It makes us want to shun or punish cheaters.

Haidt argues that in the Western secularised world these two moral foundations almost exclusively dominate our thinking. When we consider what is right and wrong we want to know: Is somebody being hurt? And is this fair? These two moral foundations are very formative in liberal Western culture. They are grounded for us in solid Enlightenment ideas like Mill's utilitarianism and Locke's theory of natural inalienable rights. In the work we have done with the Foreign

---

13 I am grateful to Rabbi Shoshana Boyd Gelfand for introducing us to Haidt's work in her preparation session for Interfaith Encounter Israel and Palestine.

Office we have observed that they tend to be primary in our thinking about global affairs. As we look at regional or national conflicts we try to identify who is getting hurt and who is doing the harming, as we are doing in Burma over the persecution of the Rohingyas or as we have struggled to do over recent years in Syria where identifying the harmed and the harmer has been more complicated. And we are looking for fairness in the international arena. We want people to abide by international law, to respect human rights and the rules of international trade. These are front and centre in Western diplomacy.

Haidt does not say there is anything wrong with these two principles. They are worthwhile and noble, but they are squarely located within a fairly narrow Western mindset that Haidt labels as 'WEIRD'. WEIRD stands for Western, Educated, Industrialised, Rich and Democratic. This category applies to a relatively small subset of the global population (it should be noted that not everyone in the West is WEIRD as current populism reminds us), so Haidt argues that this worldview skews our ability to engage in other cultures that he found to have three other equally important foundations of moral reasoning. Western secular assumptions are integral to this and Haidt is explicit in linking these three other foundations to a generally more religious mindset. I will further highlight how these moral foundations aid our understanding of the religious imagination as I set out his theory here.

The third moral foundation is Loyalty/Betrayal. One of the secularist's criticisms of religion is that it feeds sectarianism and tribal loyalties: faith-based schools can only set young people against one another, rather than instilling a sense of common identity. But Haidt argues that human beings are intrinsically tribal, as witnessed at sporting events or in nationalistic behaviour. He sees the Loyalty/Betrayal foundation as arising from the adaptive challenge of forming cohesive coalitions, connecting to our instinctive judgments about who is a team player and who is a traitor. These instincts are very much at play in the religious imagination. A major factor in foreign affairs today is loyalty to coreligionists in different parts of the world, be that an identification with a global Islamic Ummah, particularly where it is deemed to be suffering (the Palestinians or the Rohingyas), or Jewish support for Israel, or the common identity that today's Hindu nationalists feel around the world. Alternatively, it may be loyalty to forebears: to relatives who died in the Holocaust or even to colonial missionaries who brought the Christian faith to parts of the developing world. Betrayal is felt very acutely in religious communities, hence some of the most severe religious disputes being intrareligious rather than interreligious. The Sunni/Shia conflict is obviously a good example. The role that loyalty plays in the religious imagination is crucial in understanding the religious tribalism at work in the world today.

The fourth moral foundation is Authority/Subversion. WEIRD culture has an antipathy to authority, characterised by the logic that Haidt summarises as 'hierarchy = power = exploitation = evil'. Yet the Authority/Subversion foundation is crucial in most people's thinking. It makes us sensitive to signs of rank or status, and to signs that other people are (or are not) behaving properly, given their position. Authority and social order are intrinsic to religious institutions. To many people all around the world, religious leaders carry far more weight than secular politicians. The ordering of religious institutions is directly related to religious beliefs about the divine ordering of the world. And it is worth saying that this need not necessarily be the 'baptism' of current social hierarchies, as the radical politics of Pope Francis reminds us. Religious authority can be used to defend the weak and challenge the status quo as well as exploited to preserve privilege.

The final moral foundation is Sanctity/Degradation. Sanctity is a theme that might feature in anthropological or sociological discussions, but it is found in very few international relations textbooks. Yet a failure to grasp the significance of the sacred is a major blind spot in understanding the religious imaginations that are shaping the world. Perceptions of the Israel–Palestine conflict are a good case in point. The 'WEIRD' analysis focuses primarily on international law and human rights violations: who is being harmed in this conflict and who is behaving unfairly or illegally? Both of these are fundamentally important questions. But in terms of understanding the motivations and assumptions of the different communities involved, religious narratives and sacred space are essential. There is, for example, a tendency to view the controversies that rage over the Haram al-Sharif/ Temple Mount in Jerusalem (and led to the outbreak of the Second Intifada) as yet one more land dispute with some loose religious connotation. Yet its significance is entirely misread without an appreciation of the role that sanctity and degradation play in the religious imaginations of the different sides. For the best part of a millennium Jews believed that on this site, in the Holy of Holies, God's own presence resided. It is held to be Mount Moriah, the place where Abraham went to sacrifice his son Isaac. Jewish texts have always called for the rebuilding of this temple on this site and it is that theological imagination that is driving much Zionism today (furniture for the new temple has already been made). But for Muslims this is also the third holiest site in Islam. It is the original *qibla*, the direction towards which Muslims prayed before that reverted to Mecca. It is the place from which Muhammad ascended into heaven (*Mi'raj*) after his 'Night Journey' (*Isra*) to 'the farthest mosque', commonly identified as the al-Aqsa Mosque. This small piece of land is perhaps imbued with more sanctity and more concern about degradation than anywhere else on earth.

This is not a dispute about the rights and wrongs of land ownership. This is about humanity's relationship with God.

So we can see that all of this is part of a religious imagination that is of direct relevance to the contemporary political crisis of the region. Haidt's categories open up a more expansive understanding of religious literacy than merely information about doctrine and practice. He helps us to think of religious traditions as imaginative worldviews that shape the actions of individuals and communities. Without this kind of literacy to understand religious imagination we will never begin to broker a lasting peace in this conflict and many others.

FROM LEARNING TO ACTING
Dialogue

Religion is resurgent in today's world, and we all need to engage with the challenges of religious pluralism. We have discussed the kind of learning that might be necessary for this. But learning needs to lead to action. Or rather our learning needs to become active. Religious literacy needs to move beyond just an empathy with a belief system that is not your own to become a skilling in the processes by which religions can engage better with one another. This leads us to dialogues across difference.

Interfaith dialogue is perhaps often seen as something that 'religious professionals' take part in at something of a formal diplomatic level. These kinds of dialogues do indeed take place. Following much discontent at a reference to Islam made by Pope Benedict at the University of Regensburg in 2006, an international coalition of Muslim scholars, representing all branches of Islam, wrote a document entitled *A Common Word Between Us and You.*[14] This title is taken from a passage in the

---

14 www.acommonword.com/the-acw-document

Qur'an where God urges agreement with Christians and Jews with the instruction that Muslims should: 'Say: O People of the Scripture! Come to a common word between us and you: that we shall worship none but God, and that we shall ascribe no partner unto Him, and that none of us shall take others for lords beside God.' The document begins with the compelling argument that:

> Muslims and Christians together make up well over half of the world's population. Without peace and justice between these two religious communities, there can be no meaningful peace in the world. The future of the world depends on peace between Muslims and Christians.

This initiative has prompted a range of constructive responses from the main Christian denominations and Jewish groups. It has been the basis of high-level dialogues and conferences within universities and religious institutions. It has enabled local leaders of mosques and churches to come together and discuss commonalities and disagreements in new ways. As the then Archbishop of Canterbury wrote in his response, the document is 'a highly significant contribution to the divinely initiated journey, into which we are called, the journey in which Christians and Muslims alike are taken further into mutual understanding and appreciation'.[15] Popular cries in the media that religious leaders should be doing more to condemn violence and build bridges are woefully ignorant of the strenuous efforts that all mainstream religious leaders are now making in this regard.

But in a globalised world of resurgent religion, we need to move away from the idea that interfaith dialogue can be left

---

15 The Most Reverend Rowan Williams, *A Common Word for the Common Good*, 14 July 2008, published at www.acommonword.com/category/site/christian-responses

to the experts alone. The 'trickle-down theory' of religious harmony is predicated on hierarchical, well-disciplined and all-encompassing religious institutions that are largely a fantasy. Interfaith dialogue needs to be taking place at all levels within religious communities, and we will come on to consider practices of interreligious dialogue that we have found fruitful among students at LSE. But I want to suggest that the scope of interfaith conversation needs to be even wider. Our dialogues should be opened up to everyone, including those who would not consider themselves overtly religious. It could be tempting for those of a secular or non-religious standpoint to wait with impatient frustration for religious believers to resolve their differences. Yet it is not this straightforward. Non-religious and secular perspectives are very much part of the conversation, as we see in our engagement with international diplomacy. Most Western politicians and diplomats would consider themselves to be standing outside of that interreligious encounter. They would believe themselves to be coming from some neutral secular perspective. And yet this is not how most of the non-Western world perceives them. Non-Western governments and publics perceive them in one of two ways. The first is as Christians. However much church attendance may have dropped in Western Europe and America, we are still associated with Christianity. As an extreme example, Islamist terrorists are increasingly justifying their attacks on Europeans and Americans not because we are Westerners but because we are Christians. Rome has been a focus of Islamic State rhetoric as the symbolic centre of the Christian West.[16] Many people might simply think that is a distorted perception. But it may also be that they see something we do not often see,

---

16 See, for example, how Islamic State named the Vatican as a primary target, seeing it as a symbol of Western Christian power (Giangravè 2017).

which is how deeply rooted are our culture, our institutions and our value system in our Christian heritage. Most people in the West may no longer go to church. But they continue to believe 'Christian sorts of things' in their understanding of justice and values, and our culture remains shaped by Christian practices like the celebration of Christmas and the observance of a Sunday Sabbath. As we saw, this is the thesis advanced by Nick Spencer in his book *The Evolution of the West: How Christianity Has Shaped Our Values*, where he argues that even secularism as a concept has emerged out of the Christian tradition and is not present in other faith traditions (Spencer 2016).

The alternative perception that many in the non-Western world may have is that our secularism is far less neutral that we consider it to be. To create a public sphere that marginalises religion has seemed to many like a logical clearing away of eccentric beliefs and superstitions, allowing us a 'level playing field' for individuals and communities to interact. But many religious people perceive this public sphere to be far from neutral. Some may question the legitimacy or neutrality of the values and ideas that are perceived as normative in the modern Western social model, such as we discussed in the last chapter in relation to democracy, free markets and human rights. They may see them as making clear moral preferences with which they take issue, such as the privileging of the individual over group customs, the centrality of material acquisitiveness or the distinction made between public and personal ethics. They may look at the advent of 'fake news' or our obsession with celebrity culture and wonder whether our eradication of religion has really achieved the rationality in public discourse that we claim. Many people in the non-Western world see our atheist assumptions as leading to a society that is decadent, nihilistic, atomised and lost. They see secularism as laden with its own ideologies rather than as an expression of ideological neutrality.

So we need to be aware that whatever our personal beliefs we are already a potential partner in an interfaith conversation. We are all coming from a contestable position whether that is culturally Christian or operating with a set of chosen assumptions and judgments that are embedded within the framework that we call secular. At LSE we feel it is important that those who would identify as 'non-religious' are included within the sphere of 'interfaith'. Many of our programme participants are not affiliated to one of the major religious traditions. But frequently they may recognise in the course of the programme that they do in fact have sympathies with one tradition (usually the one in which they were brought up) or their own set of beliefs and spiritual practices gleaned from a pluralist engagement with different faith traditions and philosophies.

Dialogue and conversation may well be the best means of fostering religious literacy. Face-to-face interaction with people of other faiths can be the most fruitful for under-standing both what other people believe and how they believe it. It brings literacy off the page and takes it precisely into the realm of the imagination to see the world as others see it. These dialogues may be as informal as a chat with a colleague or a chance encounter with a stranger. But such conversations are disappointingly rare. Religion has long been held to be one of those topics of conversation avoided in polite company. This has been a consequence of our Western relegation of religion to private life and perhaps our experience that it can cause conflict, but it contrasts starkly with the experiences I've had in other parts of the world where almost complete strangers have been quite happy to grill me about my religious beliefs. It has been compounded by a contemporary anxiety about causing offence. It sometimes feels, particularly in universities, as if we are degenerating into a defensive and conflictual culture where making comment or enquiry about other people's identity is to invite accusations of offence or prejudice. The Baha'i student quoted at the start of this chapter is right; we have radical religious diversity at our university but people are often too nervous to talk about it. This has led us to set up a number of programmes at LSE to foster both religious literacy and interreligious dialogue, one of which is called Interfaith Buddies. It targets new students in their very first week at university, encouraging them to join small, semi-structured discussion groups with students of other faiths and no faith. They are not required to have any expert knowledge. We just give them some questions to discuss, such as 'What were you brought up to believe was most important in life and has it changed as you've got older?' or 'Do you pray and what do you think prayer does?'. Essentially, it is just giving students who are new to the university permission to ask questions and share their own faith in a safe environment where they have agreed to some ground rules, where trust can grow and where they are unlikely to be accused of causing offence.

But, of course, the reticence to talk about religion goes well beyond university campuses. Many people, and particularly those in public life, need to overcome their terror of talking about religion. Alistair Campbell expressed it well in his now famous response 'We don't do God'. Many in the media, government or professional class find conversation about their own religious or spiritual views extremely difficult, partly because many have not thought very hard about it and assumed they wouldn't need to. And they are terrified of talking about other people's faiths because our European tradition has made us believe that it will always be divisive and fuel sectarianism. Often people lack the literacy to even know what kind of believers they are talking to, and there is a fear that engaging more extreme religious opinions amounts to an endorsement of them. My experience has been that politicians and civil servants are often reluctant to talk to anyone but the most liberal Muslims, for example, for fear that their non-negotiable liberal assumptions are challenged. We are at a very dangerous point at the moment where government policy is in danger of creating 'good believers' and 'bad believers' according to whether or not they sign up to a set of liberal values that are themselves highly contested for reasons discussed in the last chapter. But interfaith conversation must be as wide as possible. What is the point of interfaith conversation unless we are willing to talk to the more extreme elements on all sides? Are these not precisely the people that we want to keep on board and to encourage that they have a stake in our shared society – both national society and global society?

If Interfaith Buddies is a 'toe in the water' of interfaith dialogue, the conversation quoted at the start of this chapter is part of a more formal and engaged method of building religious literacy and understanding through dialogue. Scriptural Reasoning is a practice that began in a few universities in Britain and North America and has now gone global, building new interreligious understanding in schools, prisons, hospitals and community groups.[17] It has redefined the interfaith endeavour for the twenty-first century since it represents an almost total inversion of the interfaith method from the forms that dominated the late twentieth century, which tended to incline towards religious syncretism. We will take a look at the syncretistic approach to interfaith relations before coming on to see how Scriptural Reasoning challenges it.

Syncretism seeks to unify different religious traditions, deeming their differences to be trivial or irrelevant. Histori-

---

17 There are now many resources available on Scriptural Reasoning for both practical use and academic study. The former can be found on the website scripturalreasoning.org. An outstanding example of the latter is Ford and Pecknold (2006).

cally, this can be viewed as an extension of the liberal Protestant project that had been going on since the nineteenth century to eradicate from Christianity all the things that made it inconsistent with modern thought (like miracles and metaphysical doctrine). Now it became a bigger liberal project of eradicating from *all* religions things that made them inconsistent with each other, as well as modern thought. As such, it ran in parallel with the liberal modern project of globalisation discussed in the last chapter, and just like that project it was far more culturally Christian and Western than its proponents wanted to admit. A leading intellectual figure in the twentieth century theology of religions was John Hick, who died in 2012. He was a Professor of Philosophy of Religion and one-time vice-president of the World Congress of Faiths. Hick was a Kantian and, following this German philosopher, argued that all theology should be understood not as *descriptions* of God but *perceptions* of God. And of course, you can have different perceptions of the same thing, like the three blind men who feel different parts of the elephant and so describe three different objects when in fact they are feeling the same animal.

That may sound quite attractive as a model of understanding different religions – differing descriptions of the same object. And there is merit in going some way with this. But the syncretist project hit the buffers, because it simply didn't take religion and religious narratives seriously enough on their own terms. Details and particular practices are hugely important in religious practice, as any vicar who's ever tried to implement a few little changes in their parish will tell you! People don't want to be told that something they appreciate greatly is an irrelevant point of doctrine or ritual or practice and they should give it up for the sake of what's really at stake. Human beings don't seem to work like that. Religion involves assenting to, and acting on, truth claims, and believers are understandably resistant to diminishing their importance.

Discerning universal principles and values is a very attractive enterprise, particularly in an age of globalisation. There are those who argue that at the heart of the religious ethic of all the world religions is the so-called Golden Rule: 'Treat others in a way you would want to be treated yourself.' And we do indeed find that somewhere in all the main faiths going right back to Confucius who said it 500 years before Jesus did. So a lot of people want to say that this ethic is at the heart of religion, a simple call perhaps to compassion. But what then is all this doctrinal and ritual detail for? We might conclude that it is just unnecessary accretion that can be done away with. That is clearly what many atheist humanists would say: we know what good ethical principles are, we don't need dogma or worship. But maybe it's not that easy. What if all this detail is in fact necessary to form our thinking and shape our behaviour in ways that enable us to live those ethics out? There does seem to be quite a lot of evidence to suggest that it doesn't come entirely naturally to us!

Under this view, religious traditions might be thought of as schools for living that shape us in numerous different ways (just as any school does) to adopt certain patterns of behaviour. And if that's the case then we might also be able to say that some schools are better than others. Some doctrinal and ritual frameworks will be better at making us good people than others are. So this is not to completely abandon ideas of universal good or shared values. But we need to understand that particularities matter both in how we understand these values and how we achieve them. As we saw in the last chapter, efforts to impose or even assume universal values quickly become a colonial enterprise, and today they are running into major problems as the particularities of religious identity push back. The Italian educationalist Riccardo Mazzeo has argued that

that universalist, syncretist view of religion underpinned a lot of European education philosophy over the last few decades; but that we are moving on from it because the more we in Europe have encountered other religions the more it has dawned on us that we cannot water them all down into a single set of values. And probably, if we are honest about it, the set of values we assumed they would boil down to were simply modern European values. Mazzeo writes 'in the past it was believed that those who were "alien" would sooner or later lose their "difference" and be assimilated by accepting those universal values that were, in fact, *our* values' (Mazzeo in Bauman 2012, pp. 1–2).

The greatest treasure troves of religious particularity are our scriptures. For the Abrahamic faiths, and many Eastern traditions too, sacred texts are the primary source of wonder and enlightenment. Their complexity cannot be condensed or syncretised. They contain passages that provoke both delight and fear, inspiration and challenge. They are, to people of faith, the custodians of truth through the ages. Many of us read them every day, and they are at the heart of our worship. So rather than push these to the side as an obstacle to interfaith agreement, Scriptural Reasoning begins with sacred texts. A theme for discussion is selected, such as justice, leadership or food. The different religious believers then present their texts and answer questions, if appropriate, about their meaning. Reaching agreement is not the aim.

A phrase that has characterised the Scriptural Reasoning movement has been 'improving the quality of our disagreements'. That may seem a modest and unsatisfactory aim. But if the future can no longer be about the imposition of universalised agreement, we must hope that it will be characterised by respectful and considered acceptance of divergent views. As a Christian, I know that my beliefs about the threefold nature of God will always be challenging, perhaps incomprehensible, to a Muslim who places such emphasis on the oneness or unity of God (*Tawhid*). I may never be able to convince them that God is most truthfully understood through these three persons of eternal Creator, incarnate Saviour and ever-present Spirit, just as they will not convince me that this thinking subverts God's unity. But we can at least try to understand one another's positions better. They may at least see that I am not a polytheist believing in three gods. I may appreciate more fully the breadth of their own understanding of God's unity. Scriptural Reasoning is a process that simultaneously improves our religious literacy and builds relationship through dialogue. It is a model of interfaith practice for our plural age in which the depth and particularity of religious commitments can be fully appreciated.

Transformation

The second form of action to which our learning should lead is collaborative social transformation. We can learn more about religion to understand people better. We can learn more about religion to facilitate dialogue between different peoples. But maybe learning more about the religious imaginations of today's world could also be a source of wisdom to address the intractable problems we face. That would be a long way from the deeply ingrained Western perception that religion is simply a private matter that can only lead to division when it comes into the public sphere. But the last chapter sought to illustrate just how devoid of transformative ideas today's political culture has become around the world. The ideas and perceived solutions that fired people through the twentieth century no longer seem adequate. I have argued that religion has become resurgent in a number of problematic ways. But I also want to argue that these great traditions that have brought much wisdom and discovery in the human past can help us address the challenges of the present and the future. Climate change, artificial intelligence, mass migration, resource scarcity – all these present global problems that humanity is struggling to address. Part of the failure of our attempts is a general loss of collectivity in our way of living today. Individualism scuppers attempts to address long-term problems that require levels of self-sacrifice and these are areas where religion has both ideas and unparalleled social capital to bring to the table.

The potential questions to explore are numerous. What might Islamic banking be able to tell us about why our financial system crashed so spectacularly in 2008? What might Buddhist philosophy be able to tell us about the high levels of mental illness in Western society? What might Christian teaching about the sanctity of the human person tell us about end-of-life care? But we will look briefly at two particular examples. The first is climate change. In 2016 the German Federal Minister for Economic Cooperation and Development convened a conference in Berlin to discuss the contribution religious traditions and their communities could make to addressing environmental concerns. He said:

> If we are to achieve the sustainable development goals set out in our agenda, we will need to change how we think and act at all levels. In the long term this can only succeed if the partnerships we build include those who appeal not only to people's minds, but who also move their hearts. Religion plays an integral part in all societies and is the most important source of values for many people. Any development policy that respects people as individuals must also respect the individual worldviews. For most people, this worldview is fundamentally shaped by their religion. (Federal Ministry for Economic Cooperation and Development 2016, p.4)

The contribution from different religious leaders revealed just how rich these traditions are in thinking about the stewardship of creation and the relationship of human beings to the natural world. Pope Francis's encyclical *Laudato Si* made an enormous contribution to that conversation, even prompting a debate in the UK Parliament. So as this German politician has shown, religious literacy is not just a matter of better understanding religions because of the challenges presented by their resurgence. It is also a matter of drawing on rich resources of wisdom on the pressing issues of our time. Both the theological ideas themselves and the masses of people who are bound together in sharing them present potential for significant transformation at a time when the secular public discourse appears to be exhausted or inadequate.

For the second example I want to return to the challenges of Israel and Palestine and the Roots organisation I discussed in Chapter 1. Any constructive encounter between Israelis and Palestinians is remarkable in the current climate. The Roots initiative for dialogue and collective social action between their respective communities is particularly remarkable in that it takes place in the West Bank where such encounters are almost unheard of. But what I have found so refreshing and unexpectedly encouraging about meeting these activists is that they do not talk about the usual topics – UN Security Council resolutions or the Oslo accords or the beleaguered peace process. This discourse has become completely disconnected from their lives and has failed to deliver for them in any meaningful way. And so they talk about the issues that matter to them and, amongst them, they talk about their faith.

One settler described why it was he had moved to the West Bank. I have heard several settlers talk about this, usually in a defiant, sometimes aggressive, tone. I knew that for the more religious settlers, living in the West Bank is a matter of returning to the biblical heartland of their people's story. They refer to this territory as Judea and Samaria, sites of many of the familiar stories from the Hebrew scriptures. But this settler had a particularly rich and generous theological narrative. 'I do not believe,' he said, 'that the land belongs to the Jews. I believe that we belong to the land. That is why I have come home to the land to which God has told me I belong. But one of the things God has taught us in history is that other people belong to this land too and our story of return must not be their story of exile. Can we all live side-by-side, equal before God?'[18]

And he was really living that out in the work that he was doing and suffering the abuse of other Israelis for doing it. There are now over 400,000 Israeli settlers living in the Palestinian territories of the West Bank. They are not permitted to live there under international law. But it now seems unimaginable that all these people could be relocated in some future peace agreement or land swap. And so this kind of religious openness, a willingness not to view religious identity as a zero-sum game will, at some point, be essential if peace is to be brought to the Holy Land. I am aware that he is, among settlers, very much a minority voice. But he speaks from a tradition that goes back to the twentieth century Jewish philosopher Martin Buber who believed that Zionism must be a bridge between East and West, a mediating force in the modern world rather than an isolationist ethic. While early champions of modern Zionism such as Theodor Herzl viewed the project as simply that of building a nation state, Buber saw religion and spirituality as integral components in promoting what he called a 'Hebrew humanism' (Buber 1976). If the Jewish state was to be created in a region of the world where Arab peoples already lived, then it must be an exemplary society of coexistence. Buber was one of the founders of Brit Shalom (Covenant of Peace), which advocated the creation

---

18 Rabbi Shaul Judelman who draws heavily on the thought of his teacher Rabbi Menachem Froman.

of a binational state. As hopes of a two-state solution to this conflict fade such ambitious and generous visions of peaceful coexistence within one state must surely be revisited.

So this settler's theological vision was a suggestion to me that rather than viewing religious narratives always as a source of division and sectarianism, we might be able to recognise them as the basis of a solution, and a solution that will really stick because it runs deep in people's hearts. Nicholas Pelham, *The Economist*'s Middle East Correspondent, has argued something very similar in his book, *Holy Lands: Reviving Pluralism in the Middle East*. To him the West has to stop viewing religion as the source of the problem and secular nation states as the solution. He looks back to the Ottoman Empire as a model of interreligious coexistence rooted in the religious traditions themselves.

> Too often sidelined from negotiations, traditional religious leaders have a key role to play not only in mobilizing public support but also in bringing to the table the centuries of experience they have in successfully managing [coexistence]... Across the region religious leaders have consistently opined that human life is more sacred than territory, and backed proposals that relinquish exclusive claims on land for genuine peace. (Pelham 2016, p.169)

For Pelham, an active religious literacy is about seeing faith communities as the source of solutions rather than just the source of problems.

In acting for social transformation through the kind of collaboration between faith communities that I have outlined, what is at stake is more than just the harnessing of a unique pool of social capital or the appropriation of some useful theological ideas to solve tricky problems. Delivering a talk entitled 'The Importance of Interfaith in Terms of Social Justice' at the Woolf Institute in 2018, Rowan Williams identified that all the main crises of our age are in some sense a crisis of the human, a crisis of clarity about what is owed to human beings, be they the victims of climate change, future generations, or victims of conflict, such as in Israel and Palestine or refugees arriving in Europe. He argued that the fruitfulness of interreligious efforts at social transformation lies in the fact that:

> religious communities of all kinds tend to have what you might call a robust view of the solidity of what is human. They tend not to think that what is human can be revised and adjusted according to the demands of a particular political or social system.[19]

It is this contribution of the robust sense of the human, particularly at a time of crisis for human rights, that a religiously motivated social transformation can bring. Religions can easily be instrumentalised in public policy circles. They are seen as mass movements of people to be mobilised and reserves of goodwill to be tapped into. But it is precisely these irreducible qualities of belief and practice that constitute the real power of religion in the public sphere. When tribalism and conflict can be turned to collaboration for social transformation, we see a form of interfaith action that truly shows the best of humanity.

This chapter began by exploring the different phenomena that cause people to experience a return of religion. I say 'experience' because for many their local reality is one of continuing religious decline. Nonetheless, through migration, through technology and through various crises of secular arrangements, we are witnessing a renewed prominence of religion in public discourse and global affairs. For people in many parts of the world religious resurgence, after decades of

19 A videorecording of the talk is available at www.woolf.cam.ac.uk/ whats-on/news/watch-rowan-williams-woolf-institute-lecture-the-importance-of-interfaith-in-terms-of-social-justice

communism or imposed secular ideals, is a genuine reality. I then argued for two responses. We need to learn and we need to act. Religious literacy is not simply a matter of learning information about the beliefs of others. It is an imaginative leap, an empathetic insight into how the religious other sees the world and their place within it. And this learning leads us to act. Action must take the form of dialogue and of social transformation. Through our deepening of mutual learning and through our collective action on the crises of our age, the return of religion can be good news for our troubled world.

Chapter 4

DEEPLY CHRISTIAN, SERVING THE COMMON GOOD

The headteacher of a local Church of England school asked if I could bring in some students of different faiths to take part in an assembly for Interfaith Week. Not wanting to present the different faiths from a watered down or syncretistic perspective, I asked four students – Muslim, Christian, Jewish and Hindu – to bring in an object they use to help them pray. The Jewish student, Yoni, (who spent a lot more time on the soccer pitch than in synagogue!) was reluctant to take part, saying he didn't feel he could represent his faith well and he didn't relate well to small children. I reassured him that we just wanted a short contribution and, since it was very unlikely there would be any Jewish children in the school, I felt it was really important that a Christian school with about a third Muslim children should hear from a Jew.

Yoni brought in his *kippah* (skullcap) and *siddur* (Jewish prayer book). 'Does anyone know what these are?' he asked the assembly. Amid a sea of blank faces a tiny hand shot up with the kind of excitement that makes the child look like he will explode if denied the opportunity to answer. 'My daddy had one of those! AND one of those!' Yoni stood there almost entirely redundant as the six-year-old boy explained to the school exactly what these objects were and how they were used. When Yoni sat down, the child sat transfixed as the Christian student presented her rosary beads, the Hindu student explained his statue of Ganesh and the Muslim student demonstrated his prayer prostrations on his prayer mat.

At the end of the assembly the headteacher came over to me, almost in tears. The little Jewish boy had started at the school six weeks before when his mother had returned to London from Israel following the death of her husband to cancer. Traumatised by his father's death and uneasy in a school where he felt there was no one else like him, the boy had refused to utter a single word until that assembly. The headteacher rang me a week later to say how transformed the boy was and how much more comfortable he was with his peers. When I told Yoni about the boy's story, he offered to go in once a week to hear him read. Despite 'not relating well to small children', he visited the school every week until he graduated.

THE REALITY OF RELIGIOUS PLURALISM

This book has laid out some major challenges for engaging with resurgent religion and often-fractious religious pluralism in today's world. The major religious conflicts may appear to have their roots in faraway countries, but our mobile and interconnected world makes the challenges very live in our own communities. One would hope that the developed tradition of religious toleration in the UK would make us well equipped to address these challenges. Yet a recent Church of England report found that many congregations in multi-religious areas are not enthusiastic about interfaith work. Rather, these congregations have become 'overwhelmed, insecure and inward-focused' (Ashworth 2017). There are, of course, some incredible examples of imaginative interfaith engagement being championed by Christian individuals and communities. The Near Neighbours scheme harnesses the capacity of the Church of England's extraordinary national network to make possible numerous interfaith projects that transform community relations. But there is no avoiding the reality that the paradox set out in the last chapter of declining churches (in most places) and growing religious minorities across Western Europe is inclined to make us feel defensive and besieged. The Church of England has sensibly shifted its focus towards evangelism and the renewal of congregations, with energy and resources targeted primarily at church growth. Interfaith work can seem to be at odds with this objective, wasting time and resources on engaging with communities who often seem to be flourishing more than we are.

This attitude is misguided. There is no dichotomy between renewing the Church and reaching out beyond the Church. There is no zero-sum game when it comes to a growing Christian community and strong, respectful friendships with other faith communities. In my own ministry I have sometimes thought of these dual priorities as *growing the Church* ('Go and make disciples of all nations': Matthew 28.19) and *furthering God's Kingdom* (described by the apostle Paul as a kingdom of justice, peace and joy: Romans 14.17). Of course the two are profoundly interrelated. We cannot further the purposes God has revealed for the world in Jesus Christ without followers of Jesus Christ! And a church that grows for its own sake and not for the sake of the coming kingdom is no church at all. But they are different imperatives. Christians are called to be evangelists, *and* they are called to be peacemakers, bringing reconciliation wherever there is conflict. Often the young people I work with find these callings difficult to hold in tension. To a certain kind of zealous Christian, passionate about sharing the good news of redemption, interfaith dialogue and the interfaith leadership the LSE Faith Centre promotes may seem like a compromising of truth and a futile enterprise (though not all view it like this by any means). A major challenge is to convince them, first, that our approach to interfaith is not of the outdated syncretistic kind discussed in the last chapter and, second, that the very real dangers of interreligious conflict in today's world are too important to be dismissed. If for no other reason, Western Christians should take these concerns seriously, since the safety and continued survival of Christian minorities in many parts of the world depend on a global improvement in interfaith relations.

These dual priorities of growing the Church and furthering the Kingdom are reflected in the title of the Church of England Vision for Education, a title I have also given to this chapter, *Deeply Christian, Serving the Common Good* (Church of England Education Office 2016). If many congregations have developed a resistance to engaging outside of the Christian community, it became clear to those of us writing this vision[1] that interfaith encounter and mutual flourishing are a daily reality in many of the 4,700 Church of England schools. I have witnessed it regularly as a school governor and on the kind of interfaith visits I have made with Yoni and other LSE students. Our task in writing this vision was to articulate a Christian account of the educational vision being lived out in these communities, but one that made equal sense to learners, parents and teachers who may be of another faith or have no religious beliefs at all. The first recognition must be that if there is any wisdom for

---

1   The group, of which I was a member, was chaired by Professor David Ford and owes much to his thinking, particularly on John's Gospel and healthy pluralism.

religious pluralism in the Church of England approach, it is not because some clever theologians have come up with a formula, but rather because the Church of England as a community has learned hard lessons through history about the peaceful accommodation of difference. We wrote:

> Over the centuries we have learned much (often very painfully) about teaching and learning, tolerance, mutual hospitality with other Christians and other faiths, and coping with challenges from the social and natural sciences, agnosticism, atheism, secularism and other quarters. These lessons (widely shared with others) have helped us to shape our approach to education, and to seek to shape settings in which we can be true to the depths of our faith and others can be similarly true to their deep commitments. We recognize that this diversity of multiple depths is sometimes more a vision than a reality, but we are committed to realizing the vision in the long term, and we invite others to join us in this. (p. 5)

This paragraph contains an important claim: that it is possible to shape an environment in which a deep Christian narrative is lived out, and where at the same time others are likewise enabled to deepen their own faith commitments. The significance of this claim should not be understated, because it is a claim about the possibilities of healthy pluralism, not just in the education system, but within the broader civic sphere. Schools are the subject over which secularists and religious groups frequently fight because they are primary institutions of the state, modelling a number of principles that we believe to be necessary for the wider public good, whether that be a model of citizenship in which religious commitments are subordinate to other civic values or one in which religious identity is allowed to flourish.

Our vision document is an explicit rejection of two claims about the public, or common, good. First and most obviously, it rejects the modern secular assumption that religion should be an entirely private matter in relation to education or any other public good. Many people are passionate advocates for this ideal, believing that children will not learn respect and equality if their membership of religious communities is allowed to take precedence over the allegedly 'neutral' national citizenship. I have visited non-denominational schools where the Universal Declaration of Human Rights is printed on the wall of each classroom and even set to music in school assemblies. The liberal order discussed in Chapter 2 is considered to be a more inclusive moral framework for civic institutions, and yet we have seen the multiple ways in which this approach is currently challenged. Second, it rejects the growing religious tribalism discussed in Chapter 1, which would want a school to meet the needs and imagination of one religious group only, closing itself off to other perspectives. This reflects the growing understanding of the public sphere in many parts of the world that permits for the flourishing of one religious group only and other religious groups (even minorities) are seen as a threat to this group's security and wellbeing.

Our vision rejects both these views to argue that we can be fully Christian in a way that simultaneously permits for the flourishing of all. With the support and encouragement of a school with a strong Christian ethos, Yoni was able to help the little boy flourish in his own Jewish identity and tradition. John's Gospel, written by a community in conflict with its neighbours, has sometimes been a quarry for anti-Jewish sentiment and sectarian Christian instincts. But it has also been an inspiration behind some of Anglicanism's most generous social visions through the ages in the writings of thinkers such as William Temple, Brooke Foss Westcott and John Robinson. In the first chapter of John's Gospel, Jesus is addressed as a rabbi or teacher (John 1.38), asking his disciples what they are looking for, what they are searching for, what they desire. In the next chapter he performs the first of his miracles, which are given a distinctive quality in this gospel as signs of the 'abundant life' that is promised in John 10.10. The miraculous transformation of vast quantities of water into wine at the wedding at Cana is an important statement at the start of the gospel about Jesus' generous gift to all:

> It was a quiet, untrumpeted sign, done for the common good of the host and guests, to celebrate one of the most universal social realities, coming together in marriage; and it seems that most of those present were not even aware that Jesus was responsible for it. Yet some, his disciples did have eyes to see it, and believed. (Church of England Education Office 2016, p.8)

This then is the model for a distinctively Christian contribution to the public sphere from which all benefit and in which some will participate more fully and intentionally than others.

> Schools are signs of fullness of life for all, as they educate children for wisdom, knowledge and skills, for hope and aspiration, for community and living well together, and for dignity and respect. Many will enjoy the wine and not recognise where it comes from; some will, with our help, trace it to who is responsible for it; but whether our inspiration for doing what we do is acknowledged or not, it is the right thing to do – as followers of the One who came to bring life in all its fullness, to do signs that give glory to God. (Church of England Education Office 2016, p.8)

The four values around which the vision is structured – wisdom, hope, community and dignity – are not, therefore, liberal values imposed with universalist suppositions but ideas of distinct Christian content, grounded in the Bible and Christian practice, but which we believe will have discernible meaning for others and to which we hope they will 'contribute from the depths of their own traditions and understandings'. The Church of England vision for education, therefore, 'invites collaboration, alliances, negotiation of differences, and the forming of new settlements in order to serve the flourishing of a healthily plural society and democracy, together with a healthily plural educational system' (Church of England Education Office 2016, p.2).

This last sentence highlights the dynamism of this broader social vision. This is not a tidy conception of a nation where matters of citizenship and identity are all resolved through the individual's relationship with the state. That approach to statehood, often associated with French thinkers such as Jean-Jacques Rousseau,[2] is heavily dependent on the role of law and a subordination of organisations and affiliations that mediate or qualify the citizen's relationship with the state. These are sometimes called intermediate institutions, of which religious communities remain some of the most significant examples. The Vision for Education presupposes a society made up of a complex ecology of intermediate institutions, each with different interests and complex histories, but all with a stake in the common good of the national community. Serving that common good is not a matter of state-enforced uniformity once and for all but an ongoing process of 'collaboration, alliances, negotiation of differences, and the forming of new settlements'.

This is a strand of Anglican thinking that long pre-dates Britain's current multifaith diversity. While an established national church is inevitably tied to a centralised state infrastructure, thinkers such as John Neville Figgis (1866–1919) argued for a diffusion of power across society. Coming from the Anglo-Catholic tradition, which itself faced state suppression (ritualists went to prison merely for wearing

---

2   See Rousseau (1997).

vestments in his lifetime), Figgis was one of the first to develop a Christian understanding of pluralism. Archbishop William Temple acknowledged his debt to Figgis when he wrote that the state:

> is bound therefore to recognise 'Personality' equal in essence to its own in all associations or corporate bodies within itself, whether they be religious, educational, economic, or of any other type. It must aim at their 'freedom' as it aims at the freedom of individuals, only claiming, in this case as in that, to be the supreme source of order in virtue of its including all other associations within itself. (Temple 1917, p.224)

Thus we have a conception of a national community made up of multiple 'personalities', communities in dialogue and negotiation with one another, and all under the protection of a state that exists to promote the freedom of this complex eco-system.

This kind of Christian vision of a plural society needs to be sold to three separate constituencies. First, of course, it challenges the secular vision of citizenship, influenced by Rousseau's statist assumptions. Secularists and non-religious people need to be convinced that this kind of pluralism does not threaten their fundamental freedoms and does not undermine the overarching rule of law. Matters such as gender segregation and the regulation of marriage practices have brought this to the fore in recent years. But secularists also need persuading that a broad religious flourishing has benefits to bring them too. The image of the water that has been turned into good wine, available for those who recognise its origins and those who do not, makes a bold claim that Christians make a substantial contribution to the public good that many benefit from without appreciating it. This is an argument that has come up repeatedly in this book in the form of the long-term shaping of culture that we owe more to Christian history and Christian practice than we are often prepared to acknowledge. But even more immediately, it is easy to demonstrate that you do not need to be a practising Christian to benefit from church food banks, free debt advice, youth clubs and so on. You do not, of course, have to be a practising Christian to attend a Church of England school.

The second constituency are other faith communities. Anglicans can say that they invite collaboration, alliances and the negotiation of differences, but do they really mean it? Are minority groups as convinced that this kind of pluralism works in their favour? We often pride ourselves in the Church of England that most non-Christian believers are grateful for church schools and the religious/moral ethos they provide. But how would we feel if they said that now they really want their own schools and resent the Anglican Christian dominance in education? The same applies to the broader national scene where the Church of England has frequently taken a lead for faith communities at both a local and a national level. But increasingly this will be challenged, and other religious communities have to be convinced that this pluralist negotiation of difference serves their interest and not just those of the dominant groups.

The last group that needs to be persuaded of this pluralist vision is Christians themselves. We have already touched on the scepticism that can be found towards outmoded understandings of interfaith work in some Christian circles. This is part of a wider suspicion that pluralism and associated words such as 'diversity' are really a proxy for the relativisation of truth claims. This is not a paranoid suspicion. When pluralism and diversity are discussed in secular institutions and cultures, they do often carry the assumption that all religious positions are equally valid (or invalid) as if there were no real truth claims at stake. Alan Jay Levinovitz observes that this makes for an easy approach to tolerance of different religious beliefs 'by asserting there is no objective way to adjudicate their value or veracity' (Levinovitz 2016, p.12).

Having experienced university myself as a place where religious positions (albeit predominately Christian ones) were robustly interrogated, I was quite surprised to encounter this culture among even devout students when I started work as a university chaplain. It took me some time to realise how damaging the politicised climate with regard to religion has been to honest and frank conversation. I recall one interfaith event on the theme of Abraham where Christian, Muslim and Jewish students all presented, very articulately, their tradition's understanding of this shared patriarch. But as soon as any comparison was made that might privilege or criticise any one narrative, there was profound and uncomfortable silence. We have taught young people to respect one another's beliefs in a way that has now paralysed the conversation.

Levinovitz is right to identify this culture as arising out of fear of causing offence or being accused of holding a bigoted stance towards the beliefs of others. And this anxiety about religious offence has spread beyond university campuses into much of contemporary society. There is a widespread fear that to say anything critical of a minority faith is to be accused of bigotry. And regrettably, the Christian majority have sometimes compensated by being quick to see attack and persecution where nothing of the sort is really intended. This has been reinforced by the incorporation of religion and belief as a 'protected characteristic' in equality legislation. It has placed it alongside other categories such as race and disabilities, and we now rightly measure public institutions by their ability to demonstrate a good degree of diversity in these areas. Diversity has therefore become a 'good thing'. Within a multifaith society it is also a good thing to monitor religious diversity to make sure that no groups are discriminated against and that the widest possible range of perspectives are brought to the table. But this need not necessarily equate to the idea that religious plurality is a good thing *per se*. Let me explain this distinction. It seems imperative to me that institutions like universities should promote and monitor religious diversity. They recruit students and academics from all over the world, and if any one religious tradition is not adequately represented at an international university like LSE, we would be missing out on some of the 'universality' that constitutes the university. But that is not the same as saying that I think people continuing to have different ideas about theology and the meaning of life is not in some sense problematic. Mine is a universal faith; I want all people to understand the significance of Jesus Christ for their own lives. Religious diversity is a fact; it is not, in my view, an ideal in the same way that the flourishing and coexistence of all different races is an ideal.

This might sound like a partisan religious perspective. But perhaps it is related to the reaction of many secular thinkers that religion and belief should not have been incorporated into equality legislation on the grounds that religion is not intrinsic to people's identity in the same way that race, gender, disability and sexual orientation might be said to be. You can choose to be a Christian; you cannot choose to be black or gay or a woman. I would argue that religion is much less of an 'add-on' than this view implies, deserving of legal protections because of its deep connection to many other aspects of our identity. But a theological way of putting it might be that we should not, perhaps, consider religion to be part of our ultimate identities before God. This is to say that Christians understand human beings to be on a journey into God. When we reach that destination, it seems likely to me that our gender, our race, our sexual orientation, even our disabilities, will remain important aspects of who we are, even if those characteristics are in some way transformed.[3] Our religious identities, however, will be rendered obsolete by the fact that we stand before the object of our faith and the mysteries of spiritual believing will be made plain. Now, as the apostle Paul says, we gaze through a glass darkly (1 Corinthians 13.12), and it is right that those partial 'seeings' be respected and protected as well as debated. But then we shall see face to face, and I will no longer want to hold to any particular doctrinal framework, let alone religious tribal allegiance.

So we need to say that religious pluralism is our reality. It is our delight and our challenge. But we need to be allowed to say that it is not our truth. And we need to be able to hold this very difficult balance between being 'deeply Christian' (with everything that involves in terms of evangelism, public worship and witness, and promoting a Christian worldview) and 'serving the common good' (with everything that means in terms of respect, dialogue, collaboration and transformative interfaith action). It is this balance that many Christians and others are struggling with today. On the one hand, it feels safer to stick with the tribe, to hold to a sectarian view that merely pushes our own interests forward and fails to allow the abundant life that Jesus promised to spill over as a blessing to the world. On the other hand, we feel we are doing good by engaging in polite interfaith dialogue that does not raise any difficult issues, including our competing truth claims. So now

---

3   These are not, of course, uncontentious questions since they relate to the theological significance that should be accorded to our embodied human identities. On the question of gender, for example, some have taken Jesus' response to the Sadducees that when we rise from the dead we shall be 'like the angels in heaven' (Mark 12.25) to infer that there is no gender in heaven. Jerome (347–420ce) disagreed, arguing that if there is a bodily resurrection, we must be raised as gendered, since there are no ungendered bodies

we need to turn our attention to the tools needed to make the religiously plural society work.

CHRISTIAN SOFTWARE FOR THE COMMON GOOD

The Canadian political philosopher Will Kymlicka has developed a way of thinking about healthy plural societies in terms of their need for both 'hardware' and 'software'. The hardware of plural societies is the institutional structures necessary in education, law, media, and so on. The software is the cultural habits that shape behaviour on a daily basis, including people's interactions with and within the hardware institutions. Both are necessary: 'Institutional structures can be quickly subverted by rising strands of intolerance, or slowly subverted by enduring attitudes of indifference. Promoting pluralism therefore requires both "institution work" and "culture work"' (Kymlicka 2017). The previous section has explored a little of what a Christian vision of pluralism might contribute to the hardware of today's society. Certainly we need institutions and systems where religious identity is of no significance in civic participation (healthcare, the law, and so on). But we also need deeply faith-inspired institutions that give space to religion in the public sphere and that allow the benefits of faith (community, values, purpose, public service) to be tools for cohesion, such as we see in many Church of England schools. But we know that not all faith schools achieve this. They can have potential to feed division and sectarianism. This will be an increasing problem as the more conservative elements within all faith communities grow. Birth rates indicate that ultra-orthodox Jews will constitute the majority of the Jewish community in the UK by the end of the century (Staetsky and Boyd 2015), and understandable concerns are raised about many of the enclosed and unregulated schools they operate. The Free Schools policy has made possible a far wider range of faith schools, including those with anti-scientific or biblically literalist beliefs. So we need to attend to the software, that is to say the kind of theology and religious culture that is shaping our faith communities and our faith-based institutions. I want to argue that two themes are helpful in shaping our Christian life in a way that balances deep expression of faith with a commitment to the common good of a religiously plural society. They are the principles of persuasion and curiosity, and I will also use John's Gospel to help illustrate their meanings in this context.

Persuasion

It should not be denied that there are major issues at stake in interreligious dialogue. Of course, we are right to stress what we have in common, particularly within our family of Abrahamic faiths. But the global religious conflicts that I have set out in this book are part of the enormous divisions that we are struggling to deal with in the world today. We seem to be in an age of polarisation and strident disagreement. In 2017 the Harvard professor Michael Sandel gave a lecture at the LSE[4] in which he spoke of this polarisation within our political culture, witnessed in Brexit and the election of Donald Trump. He sees this polarisation as related to the failures of globalisation explored in Chapter 2, arguing that democracies throughout the Western world are seeing the angry rejection of an approach to politics 'that is tone deaf to the resentments of those who feel that the economy and also the culture have left them behind'. We have seen throughout this book how religion is present within these currents in the

---

4   Michael Sandel's lecture 'Capitalism, Democracy and the Public Good' was given at the London School of Economics on 2 March 2017.

kinds of forms identified by Timothy Snyder as the 'politics of eternity' (Chapter 2), although the religious dimensions of populist politics are often overlooked by the mainstream media. So how are we to respond? Sandel argued that those who formerly had confidence in the liberal order have reacted with a shock that is now giving way to a 'feverish worry, outrage and protest'. Attacks on political opponents on both side of the Atlantic and both sides of the debates tend to be shrill and angry. But in the face of such profound social division, Sandel called not merely for a politics of protest but also a 'politics of persuasion'. The politics of protest simply wants to defeat the other side. The politics of persuasion recognises the need to be on a shared journey where opponents are won over.

We need to embrace the politics of persuasion as we build religious plural societies too. The politics of protest is everywhere: protesting at the growing number of mosques or protesting at the discrimination that religious minorities suffer in the legal or education systems. Sometimes this may be needed. But the politics of persuasion brings more effective change, and it needs to operate on a number of levels. Perhaps most fundamentally an interfaith politics of persuasion enables us to be honest about the fact that some religions (Christianity and Islam for example) are universal religions. That is to say their message is held to be of significance to everyone, and most interpretations maintain, therefore, that adherents should aspire to convert others. This is not an easy truth for us to live with. On the one hand, polite interfaith conversation will want to ignore it, embracing postmodern culture's relativist view that I have no right to say that what is truth for me must also be true for you. On the other hand, we have clumsy, callous proselytising that pays no respect to each other's venerable traditions and the connections between them. This kind of proselytising destroys pluralism, because it says that you will only be acceptable if you become like us.

Somewhere in between we have to say that, while we love and delight in the religious other who (as in the Parable of the Good Samaritan) can prove to be a blessing, we will always want to persuade one another of what we believe to be true and good. Persuasion, Michael Sandel tells us, begins with empathy and understanding. It recognises that no one is going to come round to our way of thinking unless we first make sure we fully understand their own position. Persuasion takes many forms, both verbal and rhetorical as well as in the form of action. Kindness is surely the most powerful of all forms of persuasion. We have seen this, for example, in the spate of conversions among Syrian refugees who have received hospitality from the church in the UK.[5]

But even before we talk about such fundamental matters as conversion, the politics of persuasion needs to play itself out in a myriad ways. To build healthily plural societies we need to persuade one another of many things. Many people need to be persuaded that Islam is not a religion of violence. Many people need to be persuaded that religion *per se* is not a destructive force. Many people need to be persuaded that Christianity is not a spent force in this country and that the Western European churches do not lack conviction in what they say they believe. All of these are tasks of persuasion that need to be taken up by faith communities.

But in numerous practical matters of community cohesion, any government will also be doomed to failure if it resorts to coercion rather than persuasion in its task of overseeing the health of a plural society. Recent government policy on social cohesion has often adopted a tone of coercion and presumed authority of centralised regulation. But the case needs to be made. If it is good for people to learn English, we must persuade

---

5   www.telegraph.co.uk/news/2017/01/30/muslim-refugees-converting-christianity-find-safety

them of that and support them. If faith schools need to be regulated and opened up to the wider community, they must be persuaded by those who will show them the benefits. If there are rights to equality under British law that sit uneasy with religious tradition, then faith communities must be persuaded that their integrity is not threatened by the upholding of those rights. The activities of the plural society set out in the Vision for Education – collaboration, alliances, negotiation of differences, and the forming of new settlements – are all exercises in persuasion that need to be undertaken both by communities themselves and by the state as the authority responsible for maintaining the 'community of communities'.

Two qualifications need to be made about persuasion as a device in interfaith relations. The first is that for persuasion to be well received, it is imperative that trust is established first. An initial encounter in which one party is aggressively advancing their own agenda may well be experienced as threatening and hostile. Ultimately, it's not very effective persuasion. Attentive listening to different perspectives can only occur once a basic mutuality has been recognised and unconditional hospitality given and received. If a Christian group's first interaction with a synagogue is aggressive persuasion about the truth of the Gospel, it will rightly be rebuffed. If a government's first interaction with a mosque is the disciplinary imposition of directives about extremism, it will be resented and may well be counterproductive. Trust is necessary for effective persuasion, and trust is built over time. Ideally it takes the form of friendship between individuals.

This leads to the second qualification, which is that the dynamics of persuasion need to take account of pre-existing power relations. A campaign of persuasion directed towards a religious or non-religious minority by a dominant group may well be experienced as an existential threat. This is why in some multifaith countries with fragile minority groups proselytism is banned, and it is considered best if different faith groups are basically left to their own devices. But as we have seen, persuasion is about more than just the attempt to convert, and giving up on the desire to persuade each other of anything is effectively giving up on meaningful dialogue altogether. Sensitivity needs to be shown in how our words and actions are interpreted and what pre-existing history may prevent them from being well received. The history of Jewish–Christian relations is salient on this point. Centuries of forced conversions by the Christian majority leave wounds that are easily, if unintentionally, reopened.

Persuasion is not a word we use very much in the Christian lexicon. And yet most of the New Testament is an exercise in persuasion. The entire Gospel of John was written down, we are told, 'that you may come to believe that Jesus is the Messiah, the Son of God, and that through believing you may have life in his name' (John 20.31). We can assume that the other three gospels had similar persuasive intentions. And then all the subsequent books are written in an attempt to persuade someone of something. The epistles are not dogmatic pronouncements written by ecclesiastical autocrats but attempts to show people what life in the body of Christ should look like in a compelling but not coercive manner. So the apostle Peter seeks to persuade people that Gentiles can be Christians too by virtue of the gift of the Holy Spirit. Paul tries to persuade the Corinthians that a divided church is an offence to the God who has united all in Christ. And he tries to persuade Philemon that a slave who converts to the Christian faith must now be treated as a brother. But he is clear that he is persuading 'in order that your good deed might be voluntary and not something forced' (Philemon 14). The politics of persuasion is the politics of Christian life. It is essentially a robust yet empathetic engagement in dialogue across difference, and it should also be the politics of building plural societies in this age in which the politics of protest and violence is shedding much blood.

Curiosity

But if persuasion involves the desire to get our own viewpoint heard, we also need something more receptive. We need a mechanism to overcome our fear of the religious other. The first letter of John tells us that 'perfect love casts out fear' (1 John 4.18). But frequently what we find is that the first step away from fear and towards love is *curiosity*. If John's Gospel ends with a declaration of its persuasive purpose it begins with the first disciples' expressions of curiosity: 'Rabbi, where are you staying?' (John 1.38). John, in fact, is a gospel in which the curious go far. 'How can anyone be born again after growing old?' asks Nicodemus (John 3.4). 'Where do you get that living water?' asks the woman of Samaria in one of Jesus' own encounters with a despised Samaritan (John 4.11). Curiosity is the way to truth, and since John's Gospel also tells us that the Spirit of Truth 'blows where will' (John 3.8), it is incumbent on us to be open-minded about where truth is to be found. If persuasion reflects confidence in what we believe, curiosity acknowledges humility in recognising that we have something to learn from everyone. And it has been my experience of working in interfaith relations that insights from other traditions can frequently enrich and deepen our own faith. There is nothing wrong with engaging in a little of what is sometimes called 'holy envy',[6] seeing something in another religious tradition and recognising that we need some of that in our own.

---

6   'Leave room for holy envy' is the third rule of religious understanding coined by the Swedish bishop and theologian Krister Stendahl in response to opposition to the building of a temple by the Church of Jesus Christ of the Latter-day Saints in Stockholm in the 1980s.

Our Abrahamic traditions are not fundamentally alien worldviews. They diverge on crucial matters like the identity of Jesus and the divine nature, but they have common roots and have grown in almost ceaseless dialogue with one another. Muhammad viewed Christians and Jews as People of the Book, and if St John of Damascus viewed Muslims as an errant Christian sect in the eighth century,[7] then we can at least see that the idea of entirely separate religious tribes had yet to take hold in the pre-modern era. Even during periods of conflict between Christians and Muslims there have been encounters, fuelled by curiosity and the desire for peace, that have brought people together. Paul Moses has documented the little-known encounter of Francis of Assisi with Sultan al-Kamil in 1219, the height of the Fifth Crusade. Against the advice of the Church hierarchy, Francis and his companion Illuminato crossed the battlefield between the two armies to greet the Sultan with the words 'May the Lord give you peace'. The Sultan, Moses (2009) writes, 'clearly was taken by this charismatic monk'. And while Francis was clear of his own persuasive intentions – he wanted to 'turn the Sultan's soul to God' – he in turn:

> was changed by the experience and came away deeply impressed with Islamic spirituality. In a revolutionary departure for his time he urged his brothers to live peaceably among Muslims, even as the Fifth Crusade clattered on to its deadly and fruitless conclusion. (Moses 2009, p.3)

So we should not be surprised if our curiosity about one another's beliefs and practices leads to highly fruitful and peace-building conversations.

---

7   For an in-depth study of what John of Damascus meant and how it compared with contemporary Christian views of Islam, see Schadler (2018).

This championing of curiosity as part of the software of Christian pluralism may trouble those who are aware that classical Christian thinkers considered curiosity to be a vice. In his famous *Confessions*, Augustine of Hippo speaks of the 'malady of curiosity' that causes us to 'study the operations of nature which lie beyond our grasp, when there is no advantage in knowing and the investigators simply desire knowledge for its own sake' (Augustine 1991, pp.211–212). Since the Enlightenment, we are more likely to consider an appetite for learning to be an unqualified good. We champion 'learning for learning's sake'. Nonetheless, we still see this sceptical tradition about the dangers of curiosity in plays such as Christopher Marlowe's *Dr Faustus* who makes a pact with the devil in order to satisfy his curiosity. In our own age, we continue to use the proverb 'Curiosity killed the cat'!

The medieval Scholastics' concern about curiosity (among people who themselves were clearly passionately committed to learning) suggests that we should be attentive to the *driver* of our curiosity, and it is perhaps useful at this point to return to our desired trajectory of moving from fear to love. Augustine is concerned about a vain curiosity that distracts us from important things: 'there are many respects, in tiny and contemptible matters, where our curiosity is provoked every day. How often we slip, who can count?' (Augustine 1991, p.212). Thomas Aquinas (1225–1274) is similarly concerned that curiosity can simply feed our vanity and pride. He concludes that:

> knowledge of truth, strictly speaking, is good, but it may be evil accidentally, by reason of some result, either because one takes pride in knowing the truth, according to 1 Corinthians 8:1, 'Knowledge puffeth up,' or because one uses the knowledge of truth in order to sin. (Aquinas 1981, p.1868)

So it would seem that curiosity is wrong if it feeds vanity, pride or a desire for power. All of these things trap us in fear.

That may be fear of our mortality that we mask or even seek to overcome with the frenetic acquisition of scientific knowledge. Or it may be fear of the other whom we seek to dominate by means of acquiring knowledge. We touched on the risks of this approach in religious literacy in the last chapter.

So curiosity must not be motivated by fear; and for curiosity to be the means by which we learn to love the religious other, it must be motivated by love. This is a particular kind of curiosity that requires us not simply to put the other in the position of an object for our interrogation. To be the 'inquisitor' is to be in a position of power, and while we may feign genuine interest in our neighbour we are still requiring them to conform to our categories and to satisfy our needs. The French philosopher Luce Irigaray speaks of the challenge of an encounter that simply 'lets the other be':

> Such a letting be is what is most difficult for us. It forces us to relinquish the ideal of mastery that has been taught to us, not as an aptitude for staying within our limits in order to respect the other, but as an ability to dominate everything and everyone – including the world and the other – without letting them blossom according to what or who they are. (Irigaray 2008, p.58)

Loving curiosity is an uncontrolling attentiveness to who the other is and what we might learn from them. It gives space and time for them to speak before rushing in with our own questions. It acknowledges that what will be most interesting about the encounter will not be the answers I elicit to my pre-existing questions but the insights and revelations I did not expect. This is why the question asked by the disciples at the beginning of John's Gospel is so significant. They do not ask Jesus, 'Who are you?' or 'What do you have to say to us?' They ask, 'Where are you staying?' Where can we *be* with you, to learn from you, to receive what you have to reveal to us in all its mystery and otherness. Irigaray describes these encounters as 'an event, or an advent – an encounter between humans. A breath or soul has been born, brought forth by two others' (Irigaray 2008, p.231). And what results from the loving curiosity of this encounter? Can I claim to know fully what the other person feels? No, argues Irigaray. 'Rather, I experience a more comprehensive, intimate and mysterious knowledge. The encounter, if it took place, has generated this knowledge in me' (Irigaray 2008, p.34). Loving curiosity does not acquire information about the other; it receives an insight that leads to empathy.

Working with young people in the field of interfaith relations has taught me that loving curiosity about other traditions may not come naturally or quickly. Most of us are all too conscious of our need to better understand our *own* faith and the thought of engaging with another may seem premature, unnecessary or even threatening. Ignorance is safer, and the contempt for others that thinks we have nothing to learn is much less demanding to live with. But we must come to see curiosity about other faiths as both an imperative and an opportunity to learn and to grow. It should not just be a vain or controlling quest for knowledge, but rather a transformative encounter that fundamentally enriches our own humanity. An encounter with another human being is, as the first chapter of this book argues, an encounter with God, and the parable of the Good Samaritan tells us that this is equally true of an encounter with the religious other.

I would also suggest that as well as curiosity about the beliefs and practices of adherents of other faiths, we would benefit from deeper curiosity about one another's views of the wider world and its conflicts. Insight into what I have referred to as the 'religious imagination' (Chapter 3) means that our curiosity cannot simply be confined to theological ideas or ancient texts. Religious faith is lived in the world as it is today, and, as we have seen, understanding the religious interpretations of that world is crucial to healing the divisions we live with today. One of my concerns about the British government's counter-extremism strategy in universities is that it can have the detrimental effect of discouraging students from voicing their angers and frustrations. These may be about Western foreign policy or the injustices of history in the parts of the world that matter to them. Anxiety about extreme religious views can lead us to silence those who feel they will fall under suspicion. It seems that implicit within the legislation are Western assumptions that religious worldviews combined with post-colonial critiques are almost inescapably extremist. This should not be so; and if we are genuinely going to overcome religious conflict, we need to be more lovingly curious about what makes other people angry and what they seek to defend. The story is told of a rabbi whose fervent disciple says, 'My master, I love you!' 'But do you know what hurts me my son?' responds the rabbi. 'For if you do not know what hurts me, how can you truly love me?' It is these hurts and the solidarities and hatreds they create that are imported into our communities, leading to increased conflict and tension in our own communities. We must be curious about them.

Persuasion and curiosity have been offered here as the software of a Christian pluralism. But, in the spirit of the complex pluralism I have outlined, I hope that others might recognise some truth in them, challenge and adapt them, or offer new software of their own. Just as Christians learn how to be deeply Christian while serving the common good, so we all need to go beyond the popular superficiality of religious tribalism to re-receive the rich resources of our own theological traditions. Multifaith cohesion in the future will not be a case of watered-down commitments within a secular system, nor a relativist disengagement from religious difference. Rather it will be a case, as the writer of the Psalms says, of deep calling to deep (Psalm 42.7).

Chapter 5

BECOMING GOOD NEIGHBOURS

It was the first time I had taken an interfaith group of LSE students to the Yad Vashem Holocaust Memorial Center outside Jerusalem. The visit is a particularly challenging component of our trips to Israel and Palestine. The subject matter was difficult enough to deal with, but the strong presence of young members of the Israeli Defence Force made our seven Muslim students feel particularly uneasy. Literally hundreds of uniformed servicemen and women were touring the museum. As these young Israelis recalled the horrors of their people's past, the association of Islam with the threat they had been conscripted to keep at bay made for suspicious glances and an inevitable feeling of intimidation, even if unintended.

When we came to one of the Muslims' mandatory prayer times, it was unclear where would be an appropriate space for them to pray. They were anxious not to cause offence, but our Israeli guide was adamant that provision should be made and proposed a quiet corner of the terrace cafeteria area. He and I sat protectively between them and the other diners while they performed their prostrations. Several people started glancing over and pointing the students out to their companions. I began to feel anxious about a confrontation. Suddenly there was a rapping on the glass panels that separated the terrace from the cash desk. It was the Israeli manager of the cafeteria, and he looked agitated as he hurried over to us. 'Friends, friends,' he called and pointed, 'you are facing the wrong direction. Mecca is that way...'

The Holocaust was the ultimate rejection of the religious other. It was the actualisation of a society's unwillingness to obey the command to love the neighbour, even when that neighbour had done so much to assimilate into the society around it, and even when that society professed to be a Christian society. It is now well documented how a Christian tradition of anti-Semitism helped to create a climate where the scapegoating rationale of Hitler's rhetoric could find sympathetic ears in such a way that, through bureaucratic obscurantism, mass self-deception and rampant fear, the refusal to love led down the dark path to mass annihilation. The Holocaust is thus the most egregious rejection of the Parable of the Good Samaritan, particularly in the way I have interpreted it in Chapter 1. Here we saw how Jesus is challenging us to think of ourselves as the abused victim and the religious other as a source of support and healing. At a time when Europeans felt beleaguered and victimised, they did not see a minority religious group as a potential blessing but as a curse to be eradicated. Rather than a potential Good Samaritan they saw the minority religious other as the source of their own victimhood.

Visiting the Yad Vashem Memorial on our interfaith trips to Israel and Palestine is always so uncomfortable and distressing because it is the greatest warning from the past while, as the story above illustrates, simultaneously being caught up in the charged complexities of religious difference in the present day.

So many historical allusions and analogies are drawn today with the rise of the Nazis and the Second World War that there is a distinct danger of failing to acknowledge and attend to the events of the Holocaust in their uniqueness and horror. But it cannot be denied that we are currently witnessing a rise in both explicit neo-Nazism in Europe and North America along with the normalising of a more implicit ideology of intolerance and scapegoating of the kind that underpinned Hitler's rise to power. A major challenge for faith communities today is how to avoid being either co-opted or seduced by these ugly political currents in order to foster love of our neighbour rather than fear. This closing chapter will return to the themes raised in this reading of the parable to address some final questions about how our religious tribalism can turn to a love of neighbour in which the religious other becomes the source of blessing. I will also draw out some themes from Psalm 133, a short psalm about unity between peoples that has fascinated me since childhood for the curious images with which it compares the virtue of human community:

> How very good and pleasant it is
> when kindred live together in unity!
> It is like the precious oil on the head,
> running down upon the beard,
> on the beard of Aaron,
> running down over the collar of his robes.
> It is like the dew of Hermon,
> which falls on the mountains of Zion.
> For there the Lord ordained his blessing,
> life for evermore.

Christians and Jews, of course, have much in common through shared text and tradition. But it is perhaps the practice of reciting the 150 psalms (songs) from the Hebrew scriptures that I find to be our most profound bond when

I visit synagogues. In my own tradition we recite several psalms a day as part of morning and evening prayer. They are not always comfortable to recite, often containing within them angry and tribal instincts, but always giving voice to them before a God who requires praise and not sacrifice (Psalm 51.16) and who, in this psalm in particular, calls his people to a vision of harmonious living. We will explore its simple affirmation of the virtue of unity through the strange symbols it employs of oil and dew as we consider the fourfold path of recognising the neighbour, making space for the neighbour, receiving from the neighbour, and loving the neighbour.

RECOGNISING THE NEIGHBOUR

The mentality of religious tribalism and the scapegoating of the religious other involve various kinds of reductive projection. To the Judeans, the Samaritans had become a monolithic other, 'the foolish nation that lives in Shechem'. They had much in common, culturally, ethnically and historically, yet religious disagreement overrode this commonality. The striking aspect of Jesus' encounter with a Samaritan woman in John's Gospel is that Jesus is taking an interest in her and not allowing this tribalism to cloud his judgment. 'The Samaritan woman said to him, "How is it that you, a Jew, ask a drink of me, a woman of Samaria?" (Jews do not share things in common with Samaritans.)' (John 4.9). Jesus does not just see a Samaritan woman; he sees a person and takes an interest in her. Indeed he knows much detail about her life, which they go on to discuss. In Luke's Gospel, Jesus' disciples are ready to rain down fire from heaven on a Samaritan village where they have not been welcomed. Yet it is them whom Jesus rebukes, not the Samaritans (Luke 9.51–56).

So the religious tribalism we see today has a long history. Yet we have seen how it is particularly coming to the fore in

our age, perhaps through the decline of other forms of belonging, such as national identities, or through religion's fusion
with those identities, as is currently happening in India and
Russia. There is regional specificity to all these conflicts. The
religious tensions of India are not identical to those of the
Middle East. But the most striking feature of today's religious
tribalism is its global scale. The global consumer culture
in which we live, enabled by technology and social media,
presents religious identities as if they were brands in a global
market. Just as Microsoft and Apple compete for a consumer
choice that is as much a marker of identity as it is practical
decision, so the world religions have come to be seen as global
identity brands. In consumer capitalism the commodity's
differentiation within the market is often as important as
anything inherent to the product (I buy *this* brand precisely
because it is defined against *that* brand). And tribal religious
mentalities are reinforced by the increased differentiation of
religions within a 'global market'.

Yet we have repeatedly seen how the boundaries within
and between religions are far more fluid than this. The practice
of Scriptural Reasoning shows that people of different faiths
can have common conversations about shared ideas, figures
and symbols. Differences of belief and practice are real and
should not be dismissed. Yet the strict demarcations of what
is perceived to 'belong' to different traditions are frequently
artificial. A conversation between Jews and Christians about
the Hebrew scriptures is a debate about the same history
and tradition, at times differently interpreted. A conversation
between Christians and Muslims about Jesus of Nazareth is
a conversation about the same man where different accounts
are given of his identity and purpose. Hindus, Jains, Sikhs
and Buddhists all have similar interconnections of faith and
practice. The suspension in 2015 of a professor at a prominent
Christian university in America for claiming that Muslims

and Christians worship the same God[1] is emblematic of the distortion of contrasting theologies into alien territories belonging to the different religious tribes.

This is not to downplay religious difference. On the contrary, I have been arguing for an appreciation of religious particularity and an openness to unexpected strangeness in our interfaith encounters. Conflict is more likely to arise when religions are considered as competing brands of an essentially identical product and the question becomes simply one of which brand is superior. This is a dimension of tribal thinking that we explored in Chapter 1 with the emergence of the idea of religions as genera within a species. Anthropologist Talal Asad has been a key figure in exposing the historical category of religion as a construct of European modernity that has been imposed on very different traditions as if it were a universal concept (Asad 1993). The Christian West has developed ways of thinking about belief and ritual that, through colonialism and participation in a Western-oriented global society, other traditions have felt obliged to conform to. That may be our underlying problem, but as globalisation has continued and multifaith pluralism has become more complex, different projections of what is normative in religion are going on all the time. In my experience of interreligious work, Christians may be inclined to project their assumption of religion as primarily a mechanism of salvation, Muslims may be inclined to universalise their notion of 'prophet' onto figures in other traditions, and Jews may be inclined to assume other traditions share their emphasis on community and corporate practice. All these can be forms of the *appropriation and supersession* that we identified in Chapter 1 as a major obstacle to receiving the religious other as blessing.

---

1   www.reuters.com/article/us-illinois-religion/professor-who-said-christians-muslims-worship-same-god-to-leave-school-idUSKCN0VG0OU

So the beginning of recognising the neighbour is to recognise that the neighbour is strange as well as familiar in his or her shared humanity. I cannot simply attempt to understand and embrace the stranger on my own terms whether that is the negative projections of my own tribe onto that of the stranger or the assumption that what we have in common will fall within the categories that I define. We will likely discover that we do have things in common – shared tradition, shared language and symbols – that enable us to move beyond suspicion and hostility. But that is for the stranger to reveal on their own terms and for me to receive in good faith as I truly recognise them as my neighbour.

A major issue in this process of recognition is the way in which religious identity is defined in relation to community leadership. Tribal mentalities presume clearly identifiable chiefs. A senior diplomat recounted to me his frantic negotiations with counterparts in an Islamic country in 2010 when a little-known pastor of a non-denominational church in Florida had gained global notoriety for threatening to burn copies of the Qur'an. Communications technology turned a silly media stunt by a marginal figure into a source of global unrest in which several people lost their lives. One Muslim diplomat quite innocently asked him, 'Why does the Pope do nothing about this?' Anyone with even the most basic knowledge of the evolution of Western Christianity would know that it is difficult enough for the Pope to assert authority over priests in his own church; over independent Protestant pastors in Florida he has no jurisdiction whatsoever. Nonetheless popular reductionist projections assume clear authority structures within each religious tradition and easily identifiable figureheads. This is not the reality.

There is much evidence to suggest that religious leadership is in crisis for a number of reasons. Most traditions are experiencing a crisis of intergenerational authority. This is true in Egypt where we saw that two thirds of the population is under 29. Egyptian religion has clear traditional structures of authority. The Coptic Christians have their own pope, and within the majority Sunni Muslim population the Grand Mufti of Cairo is the ultimate authority in Islamic jurisprudence and the Grand Imam of Al-Azhar oversees Al-Azhar University's vast network of institutions educating two million students, including all of Egypt's government-appointed preachers. However, the religious landscape is changing. Amr Khaled is an Egyptian Muslim televangelist ranked as the 13th most influential person in the world by *Time* magazine in 2007. Presented in the Egyptian vernacular rather than the formal classical Arabic used by traditional scholars, his shows, which include a religious twist on *The Apprentice*, reach an audience of millions around the Middle East. They are particularly popular in areas that have experienced rapid social change, where traditions have been lost and where young Egyptians are looking for new ways to be Muslim in a changing world. Amr Khaled is part of a new generation of online preachers who represent all ends of the theological spectrum from progressive (like Khaled) to extremist. As one group of commentators have put it, 'No longer do spiritual teachers require a brick-and-mortar building; their temples are satellites and the internet, and the new breed of preachers has harnessed these democratic mediums to great effect.' (Juergensmeyer, Griego and Soboslai 2015, p.43)

This is why simply thinking of religions as hierarchical communities structured under uncontested leaders is no longer tenable. The dominance of this mentality is one of the reasons why well-intentioned interfaith dialogues do not effect much change. This was highlighted in an assessment of interfaith engagement in Delhi, Doha and London carried out by researchers at the Woolf Institute in Cambridge: 'Despite the widespread consensus that interfaith actors need to incorporate a more grassroots approach, dialogue – and highly formal dialogue in particular – remains a privileged means of engagement' (Fahy and Bock 2018, p.69). Organising religious dialogues or consultations around key religious leaders is very attractive, not least because of the considerable leverage the right individuals can have. This relates to Jonathan Haidt's identification of authority as an aspect of the religious imagination that many Westerners struggle to understand. And modern technology has the potential to enhance the influence of traditional leaders as well as undermine it. Pope Francis connects with over 40 million followers on Twitter. Nonetheless, identifying who the correct leaders are in a more fluid religious environment and how to relate to those with a more ambivalent relationship to conventional leaders is a growing problem. While counterterrorism strategies in the West have tended to focus on regulating preachers at mosques and in university Islamic societies, there has been growing evidence to suggest that radicalisation is more often taking place through the internet among so-called 'lone wolves' under the influence of unconventional online preachers.

So the recognising of the religious other as my neighbour means recognising that they may not fit into the structures of a religious tribe in the way I imagined. Religious traditions are diverse, full of internal contradictions and factions. I need to recognise my neighbour's uniqueness, their right to define their own relationship to authority and tradition, and their right not to be associated with all other expressions of the faith that they hold. I will admit that in our own engagement with students of faith at LSE, it seemed obvious to build our relationships with the established patterns of religious organisation on campus: the students union faith societies, which are usually affiliated to organisations that serve as external sources of authority. Only recently have we begun to see whom these structures exclude, how dominant theological strands or cultural groups can have a quite arbitrary privilege and how questionably representative 'leaders' can skew the real picture of religion and belief within the university.

The emphasis on the blessedness of unity in Psalm 133 may appear to supplant the recognition of the individual with an absorption into homogeneity. The psalm is most likely to have been one of those connected with pilgrimage to Jerusalem, and these kinds of mass religious events often appear to be the epitome of tribalism and 'group think'. Images of the thousands of people in identical white clothes on the Hajj in Mecca or the masses of Hindu pilgrims bathing in the Ganges at the Kumbh Mala usually strike the secular imagination as a loss of particular identity, not the affirmation or recognition of it. Yet the celebration of unity in Psalm 133 is precisely in the overcoming of factionalism as the twelve tribes of Israel come together in their shared place of sanctity. Religion, as we have seen, is primary in many people's identity. But it is not the totality of identity, and the higher calling of religion is to point people to a unity in God that enables them to transcend tribal allegiances. A truly devout person is not one whose individual identity is suppressed through religious observance and conformity but one whose full humanity is enriched in a joyful interconnectedness with others, of their own faith and beyond. The theologian and LSE alumnus William Stringfellow wrote that discerning and living our unique humanity, without the idolatrous pretentions of the judgment and authority that belong to God, is the heart of the Christian calling: 'In the gospel, vocation means being a human being, now, and being neither more nor less than a human being, now. And, thus, is the vocation of other people illuminated and affirmed' (Stringfellow 1994, p.71). Faith is true if it makes us more human, not less, and if it enables us to recognise and affirm the humanity in others.

MAKING SPACE FOR THE NEIGHBOUR

Once I recognise the religious other as my neighbour, I am required to make space for them within the world we share. Building relationships between people of different faiths is always a theological-political act, because it is the sharing of a discourse, a polity and, ultimately, a space. Yad Vashem reminds us what it looks like when no space is granted, when communities are forced into ghettos and ultimately denied the right to exist. Chapter 4 explored how the multifaith space needs to be characterised by a pluralism that requires both hardware and software: shared institutions and shared culture. This sharing is not made possible through the creation of a homogeneity but rather through a space where multiple particularities can flourish. This is the critical political project for our time. Liberal cosmopolitanism that ignores the significance of place, culture and history is no longer a convincing model for diversity and coexistence. It is too associated with a capitalist elite and the marginalisation of cultural and religious difference. In reaction we are seeing the rise of an ugly nationalism and xenophobia that wants to turn the clock back to a less interconnected world. But this is impossible. While we must reaffirm the notion that particular place matters – that everywhere is somewhere – we also need to recognise that everywhere is now connected to everywhere else. Religious conflicts are imported and exported. No identity – religious, political or ethnic – can be preserved in isolation from global debates and challenges. Making a space for the neighbour is therefore making a space where the neighbour's identity can be secure and deeply held, but where it is in constant interaction with my identity and all others. The space for the neighbour is a space where we are all challenged to be persuasive and to be curious in our interreligious encounters and where the onus is not simply placed on the new neighbour to assimilate. Global space needs to be reconfigured in this way at a time when exclusive religious territorialising is gaining ground.

Space refers also to environment. Just as we are learning that religious and cultural identities cannot simply be preserved in isolation, so we are learning that the natural environment is shared too. Environmental mistreatment in one part of the world has an impact on others. So part of the theological-political task for different religious communities is to create a space, not simply where we can live peacefully with the religious other who is our neighbour but where we can live together sustainably. The opening of the LSE Faith Centre was marked by a dialogue between former Archbishop of Canterbury Rowan Williams and the French philosopher Bruno Latour on the subject of religion and the environment. Provocatively, and in a conversation chaired by the director of the School, Bruno Latour suggested that it was precisely the economic models of ownership and consumption, taught at the LSE, that have led us to ecological crisis:

> Students coming from foreign countries, at great expense, come here with a very ancient notion of commons, premodern economics, traditions and are being taught to abandon those outdated notions altogether. They leave the LSE with Masters of Business Administration, very expensive ones, with the certitude that actually you can ignore all externalities [of environmental degradation] and become really an *owner*... So I am slightly worried. It seems to me that you cannot open an interfaith place like this without producing the counter poison! (Latour in Walters and Kersley 2018, p.56)

Latour suggested that part of the contemporary project of interfaith relations is the pooling of wisdom to create a sustainable shared environment in the face of a dominant economic logic opposed to traditional religious understandings of the world. Rowan Williams agreed, positing discourses of the sacred as the basis for rethinking our relationship to the natural world:

> The language of the sacred tells us, tells me, that the category of ownership, whether with things or with persons, is *unusable*. We do not have absolute ownership of our environment, our bodies, other people's bodies, etcetera. It is simply the wrong category because in the perspective of the sacred, every thing, every form of energy and life, every person, *a fortiori*, is related before they're related to me, with a deeper more universal energy, agency, with the sacred, with God, in my own framework. (Williams in Walters and Kersley 2018, p.53)

We looked at one example in Chapter 3 of attempts to draw these strands of religious thinking about the natural world into practical efforts to move forward the public debate. But I want to stress that this should not be just another project that interfaith groups might think about collaborating on. This is at the centre of the crisis of the human that we explored. It is the crisis of humanity's inability to live in harmony with the world and to allow that world to be a gift to future humans. It is also the case that the growing resource scarcities that our world will face in the coming decades will be one of the major vehicles of religious conflict. This will require much greater attention and debate. In his work on religion and violence, Religious Studies Professor Hector Avalos has suggested that most religious conflict is already produced by scarcity of resources, either real or perceived (Avalos 2013).

It is on the themes of space and the environment that Psalm 133 is perhaps most illuminating. The unity it celebrates is linked directly to specific places, to Zion (Jerusalem) and to the region that many now call the Holy Land. At many points in this book we have reflected on the need for the resolution of conflict within that land, and Palestinians have long argued that resource scarcity, particularly the politics of water, is integral to the politics of that conflict. Since the 1967 war, Israel has controlled the water supply in the occupied West Bank and water-dependency on Israel is seen by many Palestinians as a primary means of their subjugation. Until resources can be shared equitably, there will be no resolution to religious conflicts. Psalm 133 links the vision of unity between peoples with a powerful image from the natural world. Unity is described as 'like the dew of Hermon, which falls on the mountains of Zion'. The moist dew irrigating the land is employed as a simile for the blessing that comes to humanity from good relationships. But it reminds us that this unity itself is predicated on the right relationship of humanity to God's creation. As water flows freely to all, so will the blessings of peace and unity. So the ecological agenda and the interfaith agenda must be part of the single project of making space for the neighbour and recognising our mutual belonging within a creation to which we all ultimately belong and from which we cannot separate ourselves.

RECEIVING FROM THE NEIGHBOUR

The shocking claim of the Parable of the Good Samaritan is that the religious other does not merely have the capacity to become our neighbour; they may well prove to be a blessing to us and the source of our healing. This is quite an inversion of common thinking where the religious other is perceived to be, at worst, a threat to our security or, at best, as someone in need of our pity and *our* healing. This is in part because public discourse is increasingly defined by competing claims of discrimination in one form or another. Frequently these claims are justified: both anti-Semitism and Islamophobia are on the rise, and even some Christians can face prejudice in aggressively secular environments. But a public discourse dominated by competitive narratives of victimhood allows little opportunity for us to reflect on what we may receive from the religious other.

Perhaps the beginning of rectifying this is the recognition that healing the wrongs of the past should not merely be owned by the particular community concerned, much less serve as a vehicle for their current legitimisation but should be something in which we all have a stake as part of the building of shared space. The last chapter suggested that part of our curiosity about other religious communities should be an interest in their grievances and their hurts. That curiosity needs to develop into an empathy that does not appropriate the suffering but acknowledges that part of its healing is my recognition of it and identification with it as both harmer and harmed. Only through this dual empathy can we learn from these historic injustices. For example, no one should instrumentalise the Holocaust as a mere case study for our own learning or character development. Yet organising Holocaust commemorations at LSE each year and taking students on visits to Yad Vashem have had a profound impact on my spirituality, my theology and my understanding of the human. This is all part of receiving from the neighbour in a way that enriches our humanity and helps learn the lessons of the past and heal them. Similar processes need to take place in healing the wounds of Srebrenica that have scarred the Muslim community, the massacre at Amritsar by the British in 1919 that scars the Sikh community and numerous other unacknowledged hurts that prevent religious minorities from feeling understood and prevent us from fully receiving what they have to give.

Once the wounds of the past are acknowledged and given opportunity to heal, we can move beyond a discrimination discourse to appreciate more fully what gifts our neighbour may bring. Of course, human beings are different and unique.

No religious affiliation guarantees a particular personality trait or virtue. That would be just another essentialising of religion. The Good Samaritan's virtue may be entirely unrelated to his beliefs and religious practice. So we should avoid caricaturing any religious community as enhancing our society in any narrow and simplistic way. But an appreciation of this diversity of personality is itself an important move away from tribal thinking. The Muslim students on our visit to Yad Vashem had been made to feel defensive by a perception that Jewish people in general were wary of their presence there. But the café owner shattered any stereotype in his warm hospitality and accommodation of religious difference. Receiving what strangers have to give is essentially being open to their core humanity and not imposing any of our own prejudice or judgments on them that would make us unwilling to receive. But an openness to what the individual may bring makes us open to what virtues and blessings they themselves have received from their community and in which we might share. This book has sought to explore how we can learn and benefit from the beliefs and practices of different traditions while feeling confident within our own. Practices like Scriptural Reasoning combined with a mindset of curiosity and 'holy envy' can lead us to see richness and particular insight within communities that may at first appear threatening or strange.

Our reading of the Parable of the Good Samaritan suggested that to receive another person as a blessing is to receive them as an incarnation of God. Within the Judaeo-Christian tradition, anointing with oil is the practice of recognising God as present and at work in the life of another. It is both a *making holy* and a *recognition of holiness* already present within the one anointed. Priests and monarchs are anointed to consecrate them for office but also as a recognition of providential purposes evident in their lives. Children are anointed at baptism as the recognition of the divine image and likeness present in each person and renewed in Jesus Christ. Aaron is 'made holy' in his anointing for the High Priesthood by his brother Moses (Leviticus 8.30). But this is not an action that comes out of the blue. It recognises Aaron's role alongside Moses in the liberation of the God's people, acting as spokesman of God's revelation to Pharaoh. It is a recognition that Aaron is someone through whom God can act in order that others may be blessed. So the second simile of Psalm 133, the anointing of Aaron, associates unity between peoples with the blessings that flow from anointing with oil, the recognition that God is at work in the life of another. Oil is also used in the Christian tradition for healing. We can say, therefore, that the dual process of healing the wounds of the past along with the recognition that the other – even the religious other – can be to us blessing from God, is linked to human fellowship through the symbol of anointing in this psalm. It may be difficult to imagine a religious rite of anointing those of other faiths. But it can serve as a metaphor for our honouring of God's presence within them and the healing of the wounds that divide us.

LOVING THE NEIGHBOUR

We noted in Chapter 1 that the lawyer in the Parable of the Good Samaritan does not ask Jesus the question 'What is love?' but rather the more tribal question 'Who is my neighbour?' Much of this book has also been seeking to explore the question 'Who is our neighbour?' in a world of inescapable religious pluralism, where religious conflicts are imported into our daily lives and where religious tribalism is liable to become a dominant political current. But I hope that as we have asked that question, an answer has also begun to emerge to the question of what loving relations across religious divides might look like. Love is a sentimental and overly romanticised notion in the modern world, and so my final reflections are on the nature of love and how it can be made manifest in a fractious world of religious difference.

Canadian philosopher Charles Taylor also explores the Parable of the Good Samaritan in his magisterial book *A Secular Age*. He draws on the Roman Catholic thinker Ivan Illich's reading, which seeks to resist the dilution of the parable's message into any kind of universalised moral framework like the components of globalisation we looked at in Chapter 2. The parable is not an argument for cosmopolitanism or universal human rights, for example. 'What the story is opening for us is not a set of universal rules, applying anywhere and everywhere, but another way of being. This involves on one hand a new motivation, and on the other, a new kind of community' (Taylor 2007, p.738). For Taylor, the Samaritan is not obeying an ethical principle but rather committing a free act of will that defies a social, political or religious world defined by any strong sense of 'we'.

> The Samaritan is moved by the wounded man; he moves to act, and in so doing inaugurates (potentially) a new relation of friendship/love/charity with this person. But this cuts across the boundaries of the permitted 'we's' in his world. It is a free act of his 'I'... And in so responding, he frees himself from the bounds of the 'we'. (Taylor 2007, p.738)

It is not that the Samaritan's actions are an expression of individualism so much as actions of a self that is liberated to respond selflessly to the other, whoever that may be. In the face of an instinctual response, the tribal boundaries become irrelevant.

The act of the Samaritan cuts across any form of religious or social life based on insiders and outsiders. It demonstrates that while love may be learned and nurtured within particular communities, when love is genuine it reaches out beyond conventional belongings and simply responds to the need and raw humanity of those beyond our tribe. The 'new community' that Taylor sees as emerging from such acts of love is not, therefore, a new tribe.

> It is unlike tribal kinship groups in that it is not confined to the established 'we', that it creates links across boundaries, on the basis of a mutual fittingness which is not based on kinship but on the kind of love which God has for us, which we call agape. (Taylor 2007, p.739)

In the New Testament, the word *agape*, therefore, denotes a love that is not just an emotional feeling but a passionate commitment to the wellbeing of others, grounded in God's loving commitment to us. This new community, generated by love, is called the Church. But Taylor shares Illich's disappointment with a Christian culture that itself lapses into tribalism 'and treats outsiders as Jews treated Samaritans'. The network of agape becomes institutionalised and regulated. 'The spirit is strangled' (Taylor 2007, p.739).

The New Testament conception of love, therefore, is something like an inexhaustible energy for human connection and mutual wellbeing. It was an energy that, in the first century, bound together Jews and pagans, slaves and slave-owners, men and women (Galatians 3.28). It was an energy that gave early Christians a reputation as people who, in a highly fragmented and stratified Roman Empire, were 'turning the world upside down' (Acts 17.6). So in our own time of crisis for political ideas and when democratic will seems to be behind firmer boundaries between national, ethnic and religious groups, it is little wonder that many are asking how such energy can be recovered. Political thinkers Antonio Negri and Michael Hardt, for example, have written:

> People today seem unable to understand love as a political concept… We need a more generous and more unrestrained conception of love. We need to recuperate the public and political conception of love, common to premodern traditions. Christianity and Judaism, for example, both conceive love as a political act that constructs the multitude. Love means precisely that our expansive encounters and continuous collaborations bring us joy. (Hardt and Negri 2004, p.351)

The Parable of the Good Samaritan gives the model for precisely that kind of political act of love, going beyond conventional thinking about who is acceptable or unacceptable, inside or outside, clean or unclean. It is surely an act that can be performed by any of us, of any religion or atheistic belief system. Yet what diverse theological traditions perhaps tell us is that this energy cannot simply be bottled or taught in citizenship classes. I have sought to argue that part of the reason for our current crises is precisely our attempt to do that, to universalise liberal values within a secular system. Yet the Christian tradition teaches that the political act of love comes through learning to see others, not simply as I see them, but in the light of the God who has created us both. So if, as this book has argued, there is a new religious moment, a waning of the secular and an opening for the wisdom of faith, then our challenge must be here. We must resist religious tribalism through the recognition of shared humanity before God. This is the dew and the oil that bind us to one another and to the creation to which we all belong. Political acts of neighbourliness are not merely dependent on recognising the stranger's worth in my own eyes but recognising their infinite worth in the eyes of God. And as we have learned in our reading of the parable, that kind of recognition leaves us not only capable of reaching out in support to others, but also of being willing to receive the loving support that the religious other may give to us. In this way God's love is incarnate, the tribes break down, and we are healed.

Bibliography

Appiah, K.A. (2005) *The Ethics of Identity*. Princeton, NJ: Princeton University Press.

Aquinas, T. (1981) *Summa Theologia*. Notre Dame, IN: Christian Classics.

Armstrong, K. (2005) *Jerusalem: One City, Three Faiths*. New York, NY: Ballantine Books.

Asad, T. (1993) *Genealogies of Religion: Discipline and Reasons of Power in Christianity and Islam*. Baltimore, MD: Johns Hopkins University Press.

Ashworth, P. (2017, 4 July) 'New Presence and Engagement report highlights challenges for clergy in multi-religious areas.' *Church Times*. Accessed on 8/6/2018 at www.churchtimes.co.uk/articles/2017/30-june/news/uk/new-presence-and-engagement-report-highlights-challenges-for-clergy-in-multi-religious-areas

Augustine (1991) *Confessions* (trans. H. Chadwick). Oxford: Oxford University Press.

Augustine (2004) 'On Christian Doctrine.' In P. Schaff (ed.) *Nicene and Post-Nicene Fathers*, First Series, Vol. 2. Peabody, MA: Hendrickson Publishers.

Avalos, H. (2013) 'Religion and Scarcity: A New Theory for the Role of Religion in Violence.' In M. Juergensmeyer, M. Kitts and M. Jerryson (eds) *The Oxford Handbook of Religion and Violence*. Oxford: Oxford University Press.

Barth, K. (2010) *Church Dogmatics 1.2: The Doctrine of the Word of God*. London: T&T Clark.

Baudrillard, J. (2003) *Cool Memories IV* (trans. C. Turner). London: Verso.

Bauman, Z. (2012) *On Education: Conversations with Riccardo Mazzeo*. Cambridge: Polity Press.

Bellaigue, C. (2017) *The Islamic Enlightenment: The Modern Struggle between Faith and Reason*. London: The Bodley Head.

Bossy, J. (1985) *Christianity in the West 1400–1700*. Oxford: Oxford University Press.

Brittain, C.C. (2011) *Religion at Ground Zero: Theological Responses to Times of Crisis*. London: Continuum.

Brueggemann, W. and Bellinger, W.H. Jr. (2014) *New Cambridge Bible Commentary on the Psalms*. Cambridge: Cambridge University Press.

Buber, M. (1976) *Israel and the World: Essays in a Time of Crisis*. Syracuse, NY: Syracuse University Press.

Calhoun, C., Juergensmeyer, M. and van Antwerpen, J. (eds) *Rethinking Secularism*. Oxford: Oxford University Press.

Cavanaugh, W. (2009) *The Myth of Religious Violence.* Oxford: Oxford University Press.

Chancel, L. and Piketty, T. (2017) *Indian Income Inequality, 1922–2015: From British Raj to Billionaire Raj?* World Inequality Database, Working Paper Series no. 2017/11. Accessed on 9/7/2018 at http://wid.world/document/chancelpiketty2017widworld

Church of England Education Office (2016) *Deeply Christian, Serving the Common Good.* Vision for Education. London: Church of England. Accessed on 8/6/2018 at https://cofefoundation.contentfiles.net/media/assets/file/Church_of_England_Vision_for_Education_-_2016_jdYA7EO.pdf

Commission on Religious Education (2017) *Religious Education for All.* Interim Report. London: Religious Education Council of England and Wales.

Davie, G. (2002) *Europe: the Exceptional Case.* London: Darton, Longman and Todd.

Davis, M. (2006) *Planet of Slums.* London: Verso.

Doctrine Commission of the Church of England (1996) *The Mystery of Salvation.* London: Church House Publishing.

Dodd, C.H. (1955) *The Parables of the Kingdom.* London: James Nisbet and Co.

Ellison, G. (1928) *Turkey Today.* London: Hutchinson.

Fahy, J. and Bock, J. (2018) *Beyond Dialogue? Interfaith Engagement in Delhi, Doha and London.* Cambridge: Woolf Institute.

Federal Ministry for Economic Cooperation and Development (2016) *Voices from Religions on Sustainable Development.* Berlin: BMZ Division 111.

Ford, D.F. and Pecknold, C.C. (eds) (2006) *The Promise of Scriptural Reasoning.* Oxford: Wiley-Blackwell.

Freedom House (2018) *Freedom in the World 2018.* Washington, DC: Freedom House.

Fukuyama, F. (2012) *The End of History and the Last Man.* London: Penguin.

Gardam, T. (2011, 12 September) 'Christians in China: Is the country in spiritual crisis?' *BBC News Magazine.* Accessed on 6/7/2018 at www.bbc.co.uk/news/magazine-14838749

Gaston, R. (2017) *Faith, Hope and Love: Interfaith Engagement as Practical Theology.* London: SCM Press.

Gerges, F. (2017) *A History of ISIS.* Princeton, NJ: Princeton University Press.

Giangravè, C. (2017, 25 August) 'After Barcelona, terrorists name Tome, the Vatican as their next target.' *Crux.* Accessed on 6/7/2018 at https://cruxnow.com/global-church/2017/08/25/barcelona-terrorists-name-rome-vatican-next-target

Goodhart, D. (2017) *The Road to Somewhere: The Populist Revolt and the Future of Politics.* London: Hurst & Company.

Gray, J. (2016, 7 November) 'The closing of the liberal mind.' *New Statesman.*

Guerin, O. (2018, 23 February) The shadow over Egypt. *BBC News.* Accessed on 30/6/2018 at www.bbc.co.uk/news/resources/idt-sh/shadow_over_egypt

Haidt, J. (2012) *The Righteous Mind: Why Good People are Divided by Politics and Religion.* London: Penguin.

Hardt, M. and Negri, A. (2004) *Multitude: War and Democracy in the Age of Empire.* London: Hamish Hamilton.

Hellier, H.A. (2016) *A Revolution Undone: Egypt's Road Beyond Revolt.* London: Hurst & Company.

Hibbard, S.W. (2010) *Religious Politics and Secular States: Egypt, India and the United States.* Baltimore, MD: Johns Hopkins University Press.

Hick, J. and Knitter, P. (eds) (1987) *The Myth of Christian Uniqueness: Toward a Pluralistic Theology of Religions.* New York, NY: Orbis Books.

Houellebecq, M. (2015) *Submission.* London: Vintage.

House of Bishops (2015) *Who is My Neighbour? A Letter from the House of Bishops to the People and Parishes of the Church of England for the General Election 2015.* London: Church House Publishing.

Irigaray, L. (2008) *Sharing the World.* London: Continuum.

Ishkanian, A. and Glasius, M. (2018) 'Resisting neoliberalism? Movements against austerity and for democracy in Cairo, Athens and London.' *Critical Social Policy 38,* 3, 527–546.

Jenkins, S. (2016, 8 October) 'Why cathedrals are soaring: The Church of England's unexpected success story.' *The Spectator.* Accessed on 30/6/2018 at www.spectator.co.uk/2016/10/why-cathedrals-are-soaring

Juergensmeyer, M., Griego, D. and Soboslai, J. (2015) *God in the Tumult of the Global Square: Religion in Global Civil Society.* Oakland, CA: University of California Press.

Kim, S. and Draper, J. (eds) (2008) *Liberating Texts? Sacred Scriptures in Public Life.* London: SPCK.

Knoppers, G.N. (2013) *Jews and Samaritans: The Origins and History of their Early Relations.* Oxford: Oxford University Press.

Kymlicka, W. (2007) *Multicultural Odysseys: Navigating the New International Politics of Diversity.* Oxford: Oxford University Press.

Kymlicka, W. (2017) *The Hardware and Software of Pluralism.* Ottawa: Global Centre for Pluralism.

Lash, N. (1996) *The Beginning and End of 'Religion'.* Cambridge: Cambridge University Press.

Levinovitz, A.J. (2016) *The Limits of Religious Tolerance.* Amherst, MA: Amherst College Press.

Mayes, A. (2011) *Holy Land? Challenging Questions from the Biblical Landscape.* London: SPCK.

McNeill, J. (1988) *Taking a Chance on God.* Boston, MA: Beacon Press.

Micklethwaite, J. and Wooldridge, A. (2009) *God is Back: How the Global Rise of Faith is Changing the World.* London: Allen Lane.

Milbank, J. and Pabst, A. (2016) *The Politics of Virtue: Post-Liberalism and the Human Future.* London: Rowman and Littlefield.

Modood, T. and Calhoun, C. (2015) *Religion in Britain: Challenges for Higher Education.* Leadership Council for Higher Education Stimulus Paper.

Moses, P. (2009) *The Saint and the Sultan: The Crusades, Islam, and Francis of Assisi's Mission of Peace.* New York, NY: Doubleday Religion.

Nussbaum, M. (2012) *The New Religious Intolerance: Overcoming the Politics of Fear in an Anxious Age.* Cambridge, MA: Belknap Press.

Origen (1996) *Homilies on Luke* (trans. J.T. Lienhard). Washington, DC: Catholic University of America Press.

Osman, T. (2013) *Egypt on the Brink: From Nasser to the Muslim Brotherhood.* London: Yale University Press.

Park, A., Clery, E., Curtice, J., Phillips, M. and Utting, D. (eds) (2012) *British Social Attitudes 28.* NatCen Social Research. London: Sage.

Pelham, N. (2016) *Holy Lands: Reviving Religious Pluralism in the Middle East.* New York, NY: Columbia Global Reports.

Pinker, S. (2018) *Enlightenment Now: The Case for Reason, Science, Humanism and Progress.* London: Allen Lane.

Rousseau, J-J. (1997) *The Social Contract and Other Later Political Writings* (ed. and trans. V. Gourevitch). Cambridge: Cambridge University Press.

Sacks, J. (2015) *Not in God's Name: Confronting Religious Violence.* London: Hodder and Stoughton.

Salenson, C. (2009) *Christian de Chergé: A Theology of Hope.* Collegeville, MN: Liturgical Press.

Schadler, P. (2018) *John of Damascus and Islam: Christian Heresiology and the Intellectual Background to Earliest Christian–Muslim Relations.* Leiden: Brill.

Schaeder, G. (1973) *The Hebrew Humanism of Martin Buber* (trans. N. Jacobs). Detroit, MI: Wayne State University Press.

Selby, P. (1991) *Belonging: Challenge to a Tribal Church.* London: SPCK.

Snyder, T. (2018) *The Road to Unfreedom.* New York, NY: Tim Duggan Books.

Spencer, N. (2016) *The Evolution of the West: How Christianity Has Shaped Our Values.* London: SPCK.

Spencer, N. (2017) *The Political Samaritan: How Power Hijacked a Parable.* London: Bloomsbury.

Spencer, N. (2018) Enlightenment and progress, or why Steven Pinker is wrong [Book review]. Accessed on 30/6/2018 at www.theosthinktank.co.uk/comment/2018/02/20/enlightenment-and-progress-or-why-steven-pinker-is-wrong

Staetsky, D. and Boyd, J. (2015) *Strictly Orthodox Rising: What the Demography of British Jews Tells Us about the Future of the Community.* London: Institute for Jewish Policy Research.

Stringfellow, W. (1994) *A Keeper of the Word: Selected Writings of William Stringfellow* (ed. B. Wylie Kellerman). Grand Rapids, MI: William B. Eerdmans.

Taylor, C. (2007) *A Secular Age.* Cambridge, MA: The Belknap Press.

Temple, W. (1917) *Mens Creatrix.* London: Macmillan and Co.

Voltaire (1924) *The Philosophical Dictionary* (trans. H.I. Woolf). New York, NY: Knopf. (Original work published 1764) Accessed on 30/6/2018 at https://history.hanover.edu/texts/voltaire/voltoler.html

Walters, J. (2012) *Baudrillard and Theology.* London: Bloomsbury.

Walters, J. and Kersley, E. (2018) *Religion and the Public Sphere: New Conversations.* London: Routledge.

Welby, J. (2018) *Reimagining Britain: Foundations for Hope.* London: Bloomsbury.

Williams, R. (2012) *Faith in the Public Square.* London: Bloomsbury.

Williams, R. (2016, 20 November) 'Mass democracy has failed – it's time to seek a humane alternative.' *New Statesman.*

Woodsworth, N. (2010) *Crossing Jerusalem: Journey at the Centre of the World's Troubles.* London: Haus Publishing.

Wright, N.T. (1999) *The Myth of the Millennium.* London: Azure.

Wright, N.T. (2016) *God in Public: How the Bible Speaks Truth to Power Today.* London: SPCK.

Zagorin, P. (2003) *How the Idea of Religious Toleration Came to the West.* Princeton, NJ: Princeton University Press.

Index